Francis E. Skipp
Professor of English
University of Miami

American Literature

BARRON'S

All inquiries should be addressed to:
Barron's Educational Series, Inc.
250 Wireless Boulevard
Hauppauge, New York 11788

Library of Congress Catalog Card No. 91-36014

ISBN-13: 978-0-8120-4694-6
ISBN-10: 0-8120-4694-3

Library of Congress Cataloging-in-Publication Data
Skipp, Francis E.
American literature / Francis E. Skipp.
p.   cm.—(Barron's study keys)
Includes index.
ISBN (invalid) 0-8120-4694-3
1. American literature—Outlines, syllabi, etc.   I. Title.
II. Series.
PS94.S54   1992   91-36014
810.9'02'02—dc20   CIP

PRINTED IN THE UNITED STATES OF AMERICA

17 16 15 14 13

CONTENTS

THEME 4: The continental nation, 1865–1900   44

THEME 5: The progressive era, 1900–1920   60

THEME 6: American literature in the mainstream of Western culture, 1920–1945   73

THEME 7: Cultural diversity in American literature, 1945–1980

Glossary   **135**

Index   **137**

Theme 1   THE COLONIAL PERIOD, BEGINNINGS TO 1790

*T*he Spanish, Portuguese, and French preceded the English in colonization of the New World, but whereas the Spanish came for gold and the French for furs, the English came to settle the land. This difference accounted for the hostility between English colonists and Native Americans and also for the English colonies' becoming the first in the New World to achieve independence. For the first 100 years, the English colonists were confined to the sea-coast from Maine to Florida; the westward movement to the Pacific waited until the late eighteenth century. The delay meant time to put down deep roots, and in New England to develop a model system of public education and begin the literary arts. Their culture shaped the new nation.

INDIVIDUAL KEYS IN THIS THEME	
1	Puritanism
2	John Smith
3	William Bradford and John Winthrop
4	Thomas Morton
5	Cotton Mather
6	Samuel Sewall
7	William Byrd
8	Jonathan Edwards
9	Puritan poetry
10	St. Jean de Crèvecoeur
11	Benjamin Franklin
12	William Bartram
13	Phillis Wheatley

Key 1 Puritanism

OVERVIEW *Puritanism emerged in England around the middle 1500s. Its aim was to "purify" the Church of England of hierarchy, ritual, church adornment, "superstitious" customs, reverencing the images of saints, elaborate clerical vestments—of everything they brought under the head of "popery."*

Political impact: Puritans wished to return to more primitive principles, to simplicity, sobriety, religious earnestness, personal self-control, and to a more democratic church organization.
- In its time Puritanism was seen as a radical movement with democratic implications in politics as well as in religion.
- Puritans were persecuted harshly, especially by Charles I and his Archbishop of Canterbury, William Laud.
- Seeking religious freedom (and material advantage) and fearing that Charles might return the country to Roman Catholicism, from 1620 to 1630, 20,000 Puritans emigrated to New England. Many of them were well-educated, cultured, and of good family.
- In the New World they established a theocracy.

Calvinism: Behind English Puritanism lies the theology of John Calvin, the "Calvinism" of "The Institutes of the Christian Religion" (1560). Calvinism influenced English and American literature.
- Calvin offered his own version of Augustinianism:
  1. God is a God of authority, a king and ruler.
  2. Our duty in this world is to see that God's will prevails.
  3. We discover what God wants us to do by reading the Bible.
  4. Because of Adam's fall, mankind is totally depraved from birth.
  5. Some few of us will be saved as an undeserved gift from God (grace).
  6. For the chosen few, the "elect," God's grace is predestined and irresistible. The saved come to know of their election by inner voices and by the godly spirit shown in all their actions. The damned are damned despite their best efforts.
- Calvinistic harshness was tempered by Covenant Theology based on God's covenant with Abraham guaranteeing our ability to win God's approval through moral struggle.

Education: Education became a religious duty. Puritans founded schools and colleges and established printing presses.

Key 2 John Smith (1580–1631)

OVERVIEW *Because he was the first to form a personal image from his experiences in the English colonies in America and then to write about them in vivid prose, John Smith is generally regarded as the earliest writer of American literature.*

The Generall Historie of Virginia, New England, and the Summer Isles
  (1624): His best known book, it is a compilation of materials drawn from several of his earlier works and revised.
  • It tells of a life so filled with high adventure that Smith's veracity was long doubted, but modern scholarship has validated most of his story.
  • His rescue on the point of execution by Powatan's daughter, Pocahontas, whether true or not, is one of our great legends.
  • As an individualist combining the qualities of practicality and vision, John Smith is the archetypal American.

In America: During his voyage to America in 1607, Smith felt compelled to challenge authority and was accused of mutiny by envious companions and denied a place on the governing council of the first permanent English colony in America, Jamestown. The settlers found, however, that they were forced for survival to depend on Smith. In spite of jealousy and envy he was vindicated, given a place in the council, and later raised to the governorship.
  • The general incompetence of the settlers was such that Smith in his published accounts of the Jamestown settlement provided a warning against ignorance of the conditions of the New World.
  • Along with this warning, Smith made it clear that in the New World the first priority was survival.
  • The colonists who settled Plymouth (1620) and Massachusetts Bay (1630) profited from Smith's publications.
  • In spite of the hardships and danger he recorded, he was an enthusiastic propagandist for colonization. He declared that "no other motive than wealth will ever erect a commonwealth."

Key 3 William Bradford (1590–1657) and John Winthrop (1588–1649), the Founding of Massachusetts

OVERVIEW *The Separatists ("Pilgrims") of Plymouth (1620) had separated themselves entirely from the Church of England and, following the model of John Calvin, established "particular" churches based on a formal "covenant" between the church and the individual worshipper. The colonists of Massachusetts Bay (1630), while Calvinist in doctrine, aimed at purifying the Church of England while retaining their membership in it. Many colonists were not formal church members.*

Bradford's writings: Bradford began *Of Plymouth Plantation* in 1630 with an account of the religious considerations that caused the separatist group to leave England first for Holland and thereafter in the *Mayflower* for America. Bradford continued his chronicle of the Pilgrim experience to 1650, when the original community had become dispersed and had lost its spiritual identity in pursuit of economic gain.
*   Using the language of the King James Bible he records the transatlantic voyage, the Mayflower Compact, the struggles to survive and encounters with the Indians, the power of Satan to cause wickedness even amidst the godly, and the heresy of Roger Williams.
*   The style is dignified and grave, the events vividly rendered. As history the book is excellent; as literature, a masterpiece.

Winthrop's writings: Less distinguised than Bradford, Winthrop began his Journal, *The History of New England*, in 1630 aboard the *Arbella*, leading 2,000 English emigrants to Massachusetts Bay. He made daily entries until his death in 1649. The Journal was intended as a record of Winthrop's long governorship.
*   His plain and lucid style, is neutral and non-judgmental.
*   He sets forth the heresies of both Roger Williams and Anne Hutchinson and their expulsion to Rhode Island.
*   His acquittal of misfeasance becomes a lesson on the distinction between natural liberty and liberty under law.

Key 4 Thomas Morton (c. 1579–1647)

OVERVIEW *On any basis of comparison, Thomas Morton stands in direct opposition to the principles, personalities, and literary styles of William Bradford and John Winthrop. Whereas the two Puritans came to settle the land and establish God's kingdom in the New World, Morton came to trade in beaver pelts and to live as pleasantly as possible while he was about it.*

Merry Mount: His settlement, with its great phallic maypole, not far from Plymouth at Merry Mount, was tolerant to the point of moral license.

Writings: His book telling of his New England experiences, *The New English Canaan* (1637), is written in a rollicking, jocular style, highly ornamented with rhetorical flourishes, and heavily larded with classical references and allusions.
- It satirizes what Morton saw as pretentiousness in the Separatists, their pettiness in judgment, and their insufferable moral rigidity.
- He declared New England to be a land of milk and honey whose Indians showed a humanity superior to that of the Puritans.
- His account of the attack on his log house by Miles Standish and his men is funny, but it actually distorts the facts, for Standish seized him and then turned him over to the Plymouth authorities for deportation.
- The student should read both Bradford's and Morton's account of this episode before reading Nathaniel Hawthorne's "The May-Pole of Merry Mount" (1836).

Key 5 Cotton Mather (1663–1728)

OVERVIEW *Mather was one of colonial New England's most eminent clergymen. He stands at the end of an era as the last of the "pure" Puritans. Mather strove to restore moral fervor to the Puritan community but lost the struggle to prosperity and material values.*

Achievements: He was an eminent preacher and theologian, but his greatest achievement was as an historian of the Puritan experience. He wrote 450 works and his library of between seven and eight thousand books was by far the largest in America. His intense interest in science was rewarded by election in 1713 to the Royal Society of London.

Books:
- *Magnalia Christi Americana* ("The Great Works of Christ in America," 1702) sets forth the history of the New England colonies, supplies excellent short biographies of the great founders, and describes striking instances of God's hand in the affairs of New England.
- *Wonders of the Invisible World* (1693) was written to justify the execution of 19 women convicted in Salem of being in the service of Satan (belief in witchcraft was nearly universal).
- *Bonifacius: An Essay Upon the Good* (1710) offers counsel on conduct, remarkably enlightened on relationships between men and women.
- *Manuductio ad Ministerium* (1726), a guide meant for beginning ministers, is important for its discussion of the allusive method in writing.
- The *Diary of Cotton Mather* shows (among much else) Mather wrestling with the sexual temptation to marry (for the third time) a much younger woman disapproved of by his eminent family and the Puritan community.

Key 6   Samuel Sewall (1652–1730)

OVERVIEW   *Sewall was a Boston Puritan who devoted his life to God and commerce. He inherited wealth and added greatly to it but retained through a long succession of misfortunes his humility and reverence. Before he was 30 he was devoting his energies mainly to public service. Of the judges in the Salem witchcraft trials, he alone publicly repented his part.*

Writings: He published America's first anti-slavery tract and stood all his life on the side of human justice. He is best known for his private diaries, kept during the years 1673–77 and 1685–1729. They were published in three volumes (1878–82) as *The Diary of Samuel Sewall.*

The Diary: With realism based on keen observation, Sewall recorded the daily events of a life unremarkable for the most part, mixing his often troubled thoughts on religion with comments on the weather, business matters, the deaths of his children and two wives, the events at Salem, and as a widower his unsuccessful courtship of Madame Winthrop. Since Sewall had no thought of publication he writes with an attractive candor occasionally touched with humor that exposes his human weaknesses along with his strong inclination toward the good, including the rights of Indians and blacks.

The Selling of Joseph (1700): Appealing to Scripture, reason, and hard-headed practical considerations, Sewall urged the end of slavery, saying, "It is most certain that all men, as they are the sons of Adam, are coheirs; and have equal rights unto liberty."

Key 7 William Byrd (1674–1744):

OVERVIEW *Byrd's fame as the best-known Southern colonial writer comes from his* History of the Dividing Line *and the voluminous diary he set down in secret shorthand during the years 1709–12.*

Life: He was a Church of England Virginia aristocrat who enlarged the 26,000 acres he inherited to more than 179,000. Westover, the magnificent manor house he built, was furnished to the standards of an English nobleman. Byrd writes with a wittiness that reflects his years in England, where he was privately educated and became the companion of the playwrights Wycherley, Congreve, and Rowe.

The History of the Dividing Line: At 54 Byrd led an expedition to survey the Great Dismal Swamp between Virginia and North Carolina.
- He vividly describes the terrain and shrewdly observes the white settlers on its fringes who had indolently yielded to the mild climate.
- His encounters with the native Americans, whose appearance and manners he recorded, led him to remark, "The principal difference between one people and another proceeds only from different opportunities of improvement."

The Secret Diary of William Byrd of Westover, 1709–1712: Byrd recorded his days in a private shorthand, withholding no detail of diet, health, his reading in ancient and modern languages, the routine of plantation life, his sexual peccadilloes, and his marital quarrels (sometimes reconciled in passion). He generally speaks in a neutral tone, but frequently with lively humor.

Key 8   Jonathan Edwards (1703–58)

OVERVIEW   *Jonathan Edwards was one of the most brilliant of American thinkers. Theologian and philosopher, he stood a vigorous defender of Calvinistic orthodoxy at the end of the Puritan era in New England.*

Influence: The current of history washed aside but never extinguished his ideas. They influenced, directly or indirectly, such major nineteenth century writers as Emerson, Hawthorne, Melville, and Whitman, and through these, Wallace Stevens and others in our own day.

Method: Since Edwards was a clergyman, his discourses often come down to us in the form then conventional for a sermon: Scriptural Text, Doctrine, Reasons, and Usage (applications to life).
- The argument, whether in sermon or theological lecture, is dense-textured, inexorable in its onward thrust, and plain in style.
- It often uses syllogisms to develop its careful analysis.
- So tight is the argument that every sentence invites underlining.

Ideas: Because we were created inherently sinful, unless regenerated by God's grace we may justly be damned, nor can we save ourselves by righteous actions.
- Despite this seemingly harsh doctrine, we are the object of God's love, and "The Nature of True Virtue" is love for all created being.
- The part of created being we call Nature, presents to our senses "Images and Shadows of Divine Things," and we can find there symbols of God's truth.
- Our senses are extraordinarily aided in interpreting these symbols, and especially the word of God in Scripture, if through grace we are illuminated by the content-less "Divine and Supernatural Light" that comes "immediately" (directly) from God and is the token of our regeneration and election to the company of saints.

Key 9   Puritan poetry: 1640–1700

OVERVIEW   *Puritan poetry was written primarily to set forth orthodox Calvinist Christianity. At its best, Puritan poetry is very good, but the best is not representative of the whole. The cliches of Biblical and classical literature abound, and the colonial imitations rarely approach in excellence their English models. Genuine American poetry would not emerge for a hundred years.*

Content: One article of belief, true for all Christians but given special emphasis by the Puritans, placed heavenly values infinitely above things of this world. Consequently Puritan orthodoxy fixed the argument of their verse while images of this world—the poet's stock in trade—are too infrequently introduced.

The Bay Psalm Book (1640): This first book published in the English colonies cast the psalms of the Bible into verse that could be easily memorized and sung in church.
- Its authors, learned clergymen, aimed not at literature but simply at creating a useful adjunct to Puritan worship. In this they succeeded.
- But their translations from the Hebrew, however close to the original they might be, strike the modern ear as quaint if not grotesque.

Anne Bradstreet (c. 1612–72): The well-born daughter of one Massachusetts governor and the wife of another, Anne Bradstreet bore eight children, kept her household, and yet found strength to write poetry which places her second only to Edward Taylor among Puritan poets.
- Her poem, "In Reference to Her Children, 23 June 1659," uses the conceit that her eight children are birds to describe their lives under her care. Here to a degree unusual in Puritan verse, Bradstreet employs homely imagery to convey the warmth of her mother-love.
- Her poems addressed to her husband Simon express with impressive sincerity her love for him, which is ardent and undivided by any claims of heaven.

Michael Wigglesworth (1631–1705): The most famous poem of seventeenth-century New England was Wigglesworth's "The Day of Doom."
- The poem proceeds from Judgment Day (where "Reprobate Infants" are damned for Adam's sin) to Hell itself where shackled

sinners burn eternally unconsumed in the fiery lake, and finally to Paradise where the rejoicing saved will look eternally on "God's bright countenance."

- The high seriousness of the poem and its many vivid scenes are compromised by the ballad form of the verse, more suitable for a secular narrative.

Edward Taylor (c. 1644–1729): The greatest poet of the entire American colonial period was Edward Taylor. Unlike the best-seller popularity of "The Day of Doom," none of Taylor's poems was published until the twentieth century: each was a private act of devotion.

- The best of them, his *Preparatory Meditations*, prepared him to "administer the sacrament and deliver his sermon."
- Short lyrics, such as "Huswifery," are *conceits* like those of Taylor's *metaphysical* English models, Herbert and Donne, rich in concrete imagery.
- Despite their rugged language, the best of Taylor's poems (and there are many) can be read with pleasure today.

Key 10 St. Jean de Crèvecoeur
(1735–1813)

OVERVIEW   *After being wounded in the defense of Quebec in 1759, Crèvecoeur settled in New York State and began the life of a farmer. During the Revolutionary War his Tory sympathies led him to return to his native France. After the war, through the influence of Benjamin Franklin Crèvecoeur was appointed French consul for New York, New Jersey, and Connecticut and enjoyed wide popularity in his position.*

Letters from an American Farmer: The book, published in France in 1782 and received enthusiastically in America and in France, was a broad social and moral survey of the colonies that would become the United States. In it Crèvecoeur attempted to answer his own question: "What is an American, this new man?"
- Crèvecoeur presents himself as a simple man whose letters "if they be not elegant, they will smell of the woods."
- He is before all else a sturdy materialist who is motivated by self-interest to win a "competency"—i.e., enough for a simple but comfortable life and a little bit more. He does this through the easy acquisition of land, which he works diligently under "rational laws, founded on perfect freedom" that let him keep nearly all he earns.
- God, he says, intends America to be the refuge for all oppressed peoples. Here many ethnic and national groups, with their diverse religious beliefs and political convictions, thinly dispersed in an ample land, blend into a new and unprecedented type: an American.
- Religion becomes "indifferent" (i.e., not strongly marked by sectarian distinctions).
- Children are educated at home.
- Democracy as a political concept is not discussed, but Crèvecoeur's farmer praises a society that is without rank or caste, coercion or oppression.
- Crèvecoeur concedes that the ideal American farmer in his rural community is not representative of American life everywhere. Along the frontier of settlement, remote from neighbors and unsupported by church, laws, or a community's ethos, the farmer too soon becomes solely a hunter and his family degenerates into sloth and squalor.

- By contrast, in Charleston, the most luxurious of colonial cities, the planter class lives in silken elegance on the sweat and blood of the slaves in the fields of indigo and rice, and we are shown suspended in a cage above us along a woodland path a black man blinded, torn by predatory birds, punished thus by his "master" for a crime of violence.
- In the twelfth and last of the letters, in language half delirious with revulsion at the crimes of "civilized" society, Crèvecoeur's persona determines upon a bold experiment: he will leave his own culture in the midst of its Revolution and join an Indian settlement, adopting the life of the tribe in order to live sanely at last, in utmost simplicity, in harmony with nature.

Key 11 Benjamin Franklin (1706–90)

OVERVIEW *By 1785, five years before his death, Benjamin Franklin had become the most famous citizen in the Western world. His fame was firmly based on a variety of achievements.*

Life: Self-made success as a Philadelphia printer allowed him to retire to unpaid public service at the age of 42. Thereafter he not only continued as a fertile source of ideas for civic improvements but carried his ideas into action.

- His talent for negotiation made him an effective player at home in inter-colonial affairs and abroad in England for Pennsylvanian interests and later for the interests of all the British colonies in America.
- Returning to America in 1774, he helped draft the Declaration of Independence.
- During the Revolutionary War he was ambassador to France, returning to take part in creating the Constitution of the United States.
- He was a scientist of international renown and an inventor of practical devices, some of which, like the lightning rod and the Franklin Stove, are in use today.
- From his earliest years, printing gave him an outlet for political and social satire, and a little leisure toward the end of his life allowed him to carry forward to the year 1757 *The Autobiography* (1790) that he had begun in 1771.

Themes: Franklin was a man of affairs who wrote literature not for its own sake but to admonish and instruct his fellow citizens. His themes were the follies of the times; the dependence of individual prosperity upon industriousness, frugality, and temperance; the justice and civic advantage of advancing merit over privilege; the need to center authority for our lives not in others or in God but in ourselves; westward expansion as America's Manifest Destiny and the inevitability of its rapid growth to world eminence; and justice, rectitude, and the possibility through self-improvement of finding happiness in secular values.

Method: He formed his style on the essays of Addison and Steele and came to ask himself and others to meet but three criteria in composition: clarity, smoothness, and brevity.

- Except for the more elevated style in some his papers of state, he observed his simple rule and achieved a classic prose style, mainly free of allusion to ancient writers.
- Since his writing aimed mainly at correcting society, he normally chose the satiric mode. In this he brought to bear intelligence, wit, ingenuity, and humor.
- Normally writing in a smiling, genial vein, in serious matters his pen could kill with the delicacy of a rapier.

The Autobiography (1790): Franklin's account of his life begins with his Boston boyhood, when as a printer's assistant he already was writing satire and becoming involved in the struggle with repressive authority.
- His picturesque running away to Philadelphia with little or no money and beginning there a career which soon finds him a prosperous master printer, is the archetypal story of American success and Franklin himself the embodiment of developing America.
- As a source of income he published annually the popular *Poor Richard's Almanac* (1733–1758), in which much practical information was seasoned with proverbs, gathered from the folk wisdom of the Western world, and given their classic statement. On the whole, the tendency of the proverbs was to encourage prudence, thrift, and frugality as "The Way to Wealth." On that basis Franklin has been accused of small-minded acquisitiveness, a charge his whole life refutes.
- The autobiography, begun in England in 1771, was soon interrupted by affairs of state and not resumed until 1788. Illness before long intervened and death at last terminated the writing at the point in 1757 when the author stood before the British Parliament arguing for the rights of the American colonies.

Key 12   William Bartram (1739–1823)

OVERVIEW   *William Bartram's one book,* Travels Through North and South Carolina, Georgia, East and West Florida *(1791), was the record of his explorations as a botanist. So vivid and romantic a description did he give of the Southern landscape with its trees, plants, wildlife, and native people that his book swept Europe, being translated into German, Dutch, and French, and influencing such major literary figures as Coleridge, Wordsworth, and Chateaubriand.*

The book: Despite its luxuriant, adjective-heavy, Latinate prose, Bartram's narrative reads easily and moves swiftly. The reader clearly imagines each vividly rendered scene and event.
- The lucid writing is enhanced by Bartram's excellent botanical illustrations (which, unfortunately, are not reproduced in classroom anthologies).
- Here and there, as in his adventure with the alligators in Florida, Bartram verges on the tall tale, and his coming upon young Indian girls in their North Carolina strawberry fields provides a sensual vignette that seems to idealize his subject beyond credibility.
- Usually, however, Bartram describes his many encounters with native Americans realistically, and his respect for these natives explains the safety in which the usually solitary naturalist proceeded through the wilderness.

Key 13   Phillis Wheatley (c. 1753–84)

OVERVIEW   *Brought to America as a child and sold as a slave, Phillis Wheatley's poetry was reprinted in the early days of abolitionism, and she is recognized as the first important black writer and a highly regarded pioneer.*

Life: In 1761 Phillis Wheatley came to America from Senegal or Gambia as a seven-year-old slave and was bought by a wealthy Boston merchant, John Wheatley, probably as a companion for his wife, Susanna.
- The Wheatleys recognized the young girl's talents, and she was taught the Bible and, later, Milton, Pope, and Gray. The study of Latin and Horace and Ovid followed.
- Encouraged from age 13 to write, her first poem was published in 1767.
- In England in 1773, she created a sensation, and there her *Poems on Various Subjects* was published. She was 19.
- The Wheatleys were both dead by 1778 and the quality of Phillis's life declined. She died in poverty, her husband in debtor's prison.

Poetic method: Milton's influence is clear in the blank verse of "On Virtue" and "To the University of Cambridge, in New England." More characteristic are the heroic couplets of Pope which she emulated.
- Her diction and poetic devices reflect the admired conventions of neo-classical British writing.
- We find nothing original in her forms, nor should we expect to, but she mastered her models to an impressive degree.

Themes: The Christian gift of salvation, the divinity revealed by the Newtonian universe, pride in African-American achievement, political liberty in the new American nation, the beauties of nature.

Poems:
- The brief poem in four couplets, "On Being Brought from Africa to America," is interesting for its touching (as Wheatley rarely does) on the theme of racial equality through the capacity of Africans for refinement and their equal claim on heaven.
- In "On the Death of the Rev. Mr. George Whitefield, 1770" she exhorts her fellow Africans to accept Christ.
- Her racial pride is expressed in "To S.M. a Young African Painter, on Seeing His Works."

Theme 2 THE NEW REPUBLIC,
1790–1820

*T*he Age of Reason (about 1680–1800) was an intellectual revolution founded on the work of mathematician-physicist Isaac Newton and philosopher John Locke. Newton's mathematical model of a machine-like cosmos governed by the laws of a rational God became the basis for an optimistic faith in the power of Reason over human affairs. Locke argued that all knowledge came through the senses. This theory led to the idea that all men are created equal, since inequalities can arise only after birth from differences in sense experiences. Locke further argued that man in a natural state, acting in harmony with God's rational laws, agreed to self-government through a Social Contract aimed at protecting the rights and property of each individual. Having surrendered some of his freedom in return for this security, natural man was therefore entitled to overthrow a government that did not fulfill the contract. Upon this widely accepted idea, the American colonists based their right to revolution.

INDIVIDUAL KEYS IN THIS THEME

14	Thomas Paine
15	Thomas Jefferson
16	*The Federalist:* Alexander Hamilton and James Madison

Key 14 Thomas Paine (1737–1809)

OVERVIEW *Born of poor Quaker parents near London, Paine met Benjamin Franklin while still in England. With a letter of recommendation from Franklin, Paine arrived in Philadelphia in 1774. Paine's radical writings contributed to enthusiasm for the American Revolution.*

In America: Paine's arrival from England in 1774 was at a time when America was badly divided on the course to take toward Great Britain and its oppressive colonial policies.
- Convinced that the colonies must immediately declare their independence, in January, 1776 he published *Common Sense*, an enormously popular pamphlet that coalesced American opinion in favor of revolution.
- During the war years his 16 essays comprising *The American Crisis* (1776–83) stiffened American morale and addressed a succession of war-caused problems.

Later works: Returning to England, he attacked in *The Rights of Man* (1791–92) the institution of hereditary monarchy and set forth a program for world revolution.
- He fled to France to avoid prosecution.
- In *The Age of Reason* (1794–96) he examined Christian belief in the light of reason and advanced the ideas of deism.
- *The Rights of Man* defends the French Revolution against the attacks of Edmund Burke.
- Returning to America and widely denounced as an atheist, he spent his last few years in poverty and disfavor.

Key 15   Thomas Jefferson (1743–1826)

OVERVIEW   *Jefferson is generally conceded to be the greatest of the philosopher-statesmen who founded the United States of America. He defined our national ideology, formulated sound theories of government, and possessed a marked talent for putting theory into practice.*

Principal ideas:
- All people are created equal and given at birth certain irrevocable rights and powers including equality of opportunity and the ability to distinguish right from wrong.
- Government is a social contract between rulers and the ruled.
- The right of freedom depends for its preservation on an educated people who control their own government.
- Such a society to succeed must be enlightened morally.
- All ideas, all beliefs are subject to validation by Reason.
- Belief in God does not depend solely upon the revelations of Judeo-Christian scripture.

Method: Jefferson wrote in order to communicate. Except where his style is elevated to match the dignity of certain state documents it is plain and unadorned. He wrote, nevertheless, with a naturally flowing line, and his authorship of the Declaration of Independence established him as the best writer in the patriotic cause.

Declaration of Independence: When approved by the Continental Congress on July 4, 1776, the Declaration of Independence divorced the British colonies in North America from Great Britain and established as a new nation the United States of America. Its argument:
- The God-given right to "life, liberty, and the pursuit of happiness" can be enjoyed only if protected by government.
- The right of a government to exist rests on the social contract.
- A government may be renounced when the people find this contract broken, their rights abused.

Notes on the State of Virginia (1784–85): These were informal though serious replies to 23 queries sent to Jefferson by the secretary of the French legation in Philadelphia. They are concerned with topography, zoology, anthropology, economics, religion, and other matters.
- In describing the **Natural Bridge** Jefferson speaks in terms of "the sublime"—terror, wonder, and awe.
- In his reply to **Query VI**, Jefferson refutes the assertion of the

famous French naturalist, the Count de Buffon, that Native Americans are inferior human beings, that the animals are smaller than European examples of the same species, and that European animals brought to the New World degenerate in the new environment.

- Responding to **Query XVII, Religion**, Jefferson declares that the laws of the United States have wiped away all previously established oppressive religious statutes, that free enquiry can dispose of all questions of heresy, and that religious disputes in America are silenced by being ignored.
- With respect to **Manufactures**, America avoids the evils of industrialization by preferring to supply Europe with raw materials and receiving back finished products (a preference he modified during the Napoleonic War).
- **Slavery** he declared to be contrary to God's will, and he says that the slaves should be emancipated in an orderly way before God's wrath settles the issue violently.

Letters:
- To young Peter Carr Jefferson offers educational advice:
  1. foreign languages should be acquired for their practical value (therefore Spanish rather than Italian);
  2. everyone possesses moral sense naturally, so courses in moral philosophy are useless;
  3. for religion read the Bible, religious histories (especially lives of Christ), accepting nothing that calm Reason does not approve; and
  4. travel interferes with a young person's natural development.
- Responding to Benjamin Rush, Jefferson says that Jesus claimed only *human*, not divine attributes. His short life allowed too little time for him to develop a complete system of morals, but what he left us is incomparable.
- John Adams and Jefferson corresponded extensively in their retirement. In one letter Jefferson argues that the aristocracy that Adams favored was artificial, based as it was on birth and wealth, and advanced the idea of a natural aristocracy based solely on merit. In another letter Jefferson bases his belief in God on the complexity and magnitude of the design of the cosmos ("argument from design") and declares that the extinction of species on earth and of stars in the heavens points to "an eternal preexistence of a creator rather than that of a self-existent universe."

First Inaugural Address: Calls for faith in representative government under law. Asserts the right of the majority will to prevail, but cautions that minority rights must be protected.

Key 16   The Federalist (1787–88):

Alexander Hamilton and

James Madison

OVERVIEW   *The 85 essays comprising* The Federalist *were written severally by Alexander Hamilton, James Madison, and John Jay. Each, for anonymity, was signed "Publius." They aimed at persuading New York, where opinion was much divided, to ratify the new constitution.*

Argument: The conservative authors declared "liberty, dignity, and happiness" to be natural rights and acknowledged that the Revolution had, in effect, authorized a government that should be popular in both form and spirit. But at the same time, they feared the "tyranny of the majority," and argued that minority rights must be safeguarded.
- The proposed constitution with its distribution of powers among legislature, judiciary, and executive, they declared, each branch acting as an ongoing check and counterweight to the others, offered the best structure for achieving and maintaining the interests of all in the balance essential to the life of a democracy.
- And the new constitution, recognizing that the national interest could be frustrated if too much power were to be retained by the individual states, provided for a federal government with strength adequate to preserve the balance among contending interests.
- *The Federalist* was a summation of American conservative thought and, with ratification accomplished, came to have almost the authority of constitutional law.

THE FLOWERING
OF AMERICAN
ROMANTICISM, 1820–65

*A*merican literary Romanticism derives mainly from the
English Romantic poets, particularly Coleridge and
Wordsworth, and from German Romantic philosophy.
Jonathan Edwards, in "A Divine and Supernatural Light"
and "Images and Shadows of Divine Things" is a native
source.

There are five principal Romantic themes in American
literature:

1. intuition ("the truth of the heart") is more trustworthy
   than reason;
2. to express deeply felt experience is more valuable
   than to elaborate universal principles;
3. the individual is at the center of life and God is at
   the center of the individual;
4. nature is an array of physical symbols from which
   knowledge of the supernatural can be intuited; and
5. we should aspire to the Ideal, to changing what is to
   what ought to be.

Emerson is the most comprehensive and influential
spokesman for the five principles. His book *Nature* (1836)
and his essay "Self Reliance," are the most important expres-
sions of his Romanticism. His powerful influence on Walt
Whitman is clearly seen in *Song of Myself*, the key to understanding *Leaves of Grass*. Herman Melville, like his fellow
Romantic, Nathaniel Hawthorne, did not accept Emerson
without reservation, but *Moby Dick* (1851) treats Nature as
a source of metaphysical truth, as does Henry David
Thoreau, Emerson's protége and William Cullen Bryant,

whose best poems antedate Emerson's influence. Edgar Allan Poe stands outside this group, but his poems and best tales aim at arousing the Romantic emotions of the "sublime"—terror, wonder and awe.

INDIVIDUAL KEYS IN THIS THEME	
17	Washington Irving
18	James Fenimore Cooper
19	William Cullen Bryant
20	Transcendentalism
21	Ralph Waldo Emerson
22	Margaret Fuller
23	Nathaniel Hawthorne
24	Longfellow, Whittier, Lowell, Holmes
25	Edgar Allan Poe
26	Henry David Thoreau
27	Herman Melville
28	Walt Whitman
29	Harriet Beecher Stowe
30	Frederick Douglass
31	Humor of the frontier

Key 17 Washington Irving (1783–1859)

OVERVIEW *Irving was America's first classic writer. His best work was admired for its high finish and perfection of expression, for delicately tinted scene-painting, for genial humor, and for three or four unforgettable characters it lodged in our national consciousness. Irving influenced such classic American writers as his admirers Poe and Hawthorne, and he is pleasurably read today. Through Irving, American writing as art came into being.*

Narrative method: For his best work, Irving took German folk tales or Spanish legends and recast them.
- He gave the spare old tales such picturesque color and human richness as to transform them utterly.
- He wrote with great care and diligently polished what he had written to achieve the tone that distinguishes his best work.

Satire: Irving's first important book was *A History of New York from the Beginning of the World to the End of the Dutch Dynasty* (1809), a title characteristic of Irving's droll manner. He pretended that the author was one Diedrich Knickerbocker.
- The Dutch colonials are presented with genial hilarity as absurd and grotesque in this mock-epic.
- Yankees and Swedes are the objects of the same comic satire.

Tales: Irving wrote four books of tales, the two major ones being *The Sketch Book of Geoffrey Crayon, Gent.* (1819–20) and *Tales of the Alhambra* (1832)—his so-called "Spanish *Sketch Book*." Two tales from the former have made Irving immortal: "Rip Van Winkle" and "The Legend of Sleepy Hollow."
- In this Americanization of medieval Germanic myth, Rip is sometimes seen as the paradigm of the American male who grows old but not up, remaining boyish and irresponsible to the end.
- "The Legend of Sleepy Hollow," also of German origin, has Ichabod Crane, an ill-educated superstitious Connecticut schoolmaster among the complacent Dutch. Dreaming of Katrina, heiress to the rich Van Tassel acres, Ichabod is no match for burly Brom Bones, night-riding prankster. Making a characteristic American choice, Katrina marries material power, Brom Bones, rejecting the intellect, Ichabod, grotesque representative of what mind and spirit there was in Sleepy Hollow.

Key 18   James Fenimore Cooper
(1789–1851)

OVERVIEW   *James Fenimore Cooper was America's first major novelist. His passion for his subject matter overrode his conservative bias and the defects of his literary style. His personal involvement in the social issues of his day left rich data for the historian. His story-telling talent took for materials the frontier, the wilderness beyond, and the sea, creating romances often touched with power and beauty. The five Leatherstocking tales and Natty Bumppo, the woodsman who links them all, are his strongest claim on immortality.*

Narrative method: Cooper adopted the form of the English novel of his time.
- His tales depend on the well-worn devices of flight and pursuit, of struggle for possession of neutral ground, of capture and rescue, of mistaken identity or concealed traits of character, of good Indians and bad, the courtship of conventional ladies and gentlemen, the deeds of strongly drawn villains, and so on.
- As this dependency suggests, the novels are filled with action and suspense, of progress and reverse, recognition and surprise, and ultimately a happy ending, not unmixed with pathos.
- The style is wordy, often stilted, self-consciously genteel, and humorless. His best work succeeds in spite of these chronic faults.

Themes: He believed that different psychological traits distinguish the white man and the Indian, traits he designated "gifts," valuing both red and white "gifts" equally.
- He expressed enthusiasm for civilizing the wilderness while at the same time deploring the spoliation of the virgin land.
- Despite this inconsistency, he was a champion of conservation, and toward this and other goals he called for leadership by an aristocracy of worth whose stability rested upon the sanctity of property and whose social justice was a consequence of patriotism.

Novels: Cooper wrote thirty-two novels, the best of which are the five Leatherstocking tales; the first two of the Littlepage Trilogy, *Satanstoe* (1845) and *The Chainbearer* (1845); and three sea tales, *The Red Rover* (1828), *Wing and Wing* (1842) and *The Water-Witch* (1831).

Key 19 William Cullen Bryant
(1798–1878)

OVERVIEW *Bryant in his twenties left the rural scenes and Puritan conservatism of western Massachusetts for New York City. He produced a small body of verse of a distinction that made him America's first major poet.*

Poetic method: With "Thanatopsis" ("a view of death"), influenced strongly by England's "Graveyard School" of poets, Bryant abandoned the heroic couplets of his juvenile work to adopt blank verse. Thereafter he wrote much of his poetry in this form, together with carefully rhymed lyrics in stanzaic forms varying little from those used by his English predecessors.
- His style is elevated and dignified, his blank verse of a supple variety within the regularity of the form.
- This practice accords with his own critical theory which also demands of the poet a clarity of statement making no intellectual demands which would interfere with poetry's goal, the awakening of emotion.

Poems and themes:
- "Thanatopsis" (1814) dispels fear by assuring us that in death personality is extinguished and the body is mixed with the earth where we join all who have preceded us, the best and wisest among them, in "the great tomb of man."
- "The Yellow Violet" (1815), the cheerful flower that marks the end of winter and is forgotten amidst the brilliance of later blooms uses nature to teach that we owe our early friends a debt not to be forgotten.
- Confidence in God's beneficent guidance through the pathless course of our lives is encouraged by a picture of the unerring flight of a migratory bird in "To a Waterfowl" (1815).
- Religious feeling as an archetypal human response to God's presence everywhere in nature is the theme of "A Forest Hymn" (1825).
- Civilizations, says "The Prairies" (1833), succeed one another endlessly, the record of their existence all but obliterated by time, just as our advancing civilization will lapse at last into an unpeopled wilderness.

Key 20 Transcendentalism

OVERVIEW *In its connection with American literature, transcendentalism designates a belief that the visible world, observed by an intuitive imagination, offers endless clues and hints about the invisible world whose truths stand eternally behind the physical facts perceived by the five senses.*

American transcendentalism: Although it has strong connections with English, European, and oriental philosophy, its native roots are to be found in the Quaker "inner light," the Puritan "divine and supernatural light," and in the secular egalitarianism fostered by the American Revolution.

- Emerging around 1815, transcendentalism found its first and best published statement in *Nature* (1836), by Ralph Waldo Emerson.
- As a cluster of ideas, transcendentalism reoriented American literature in such a decisive way as to bring about a body of work, principally by Emerson, Thoreau, and Whitman, its proponents, and by Hawthorne and Melville, its skeptical critics, of such classical excellence and unprecedented maturity as to have merited being called in later years the "The American Renaissance."
- Transcendentalism proposed the view that each object could be viewed as a miniature version of the entire universe.
- The movement placed its faith in the intuition of individuals.

Key 21 Ralph Waldo Emerson (1803–82)

OVERVIEW: *Emerson had an immense influence on the life and thought of nineteenthth century America, an influence that continues into the present.*

Ideas: He was convinced that everything in nature had its exact counterpart in the mind. From this basic conviction flowed all his ideas.
- Nature was a vast array of symbols, which could lead their individual interpreter toward the eternal truth of God and the cosmos.
- The method of interpretation called for an intuitive leap without rational analysis from the thing observed in nature to the spiritual (moral) truth it symbolized.
- Since such ultimate truth transcended nature or lay behind it, the intuitive means of discovering it was transcendental.
- Emerson did not invent this ancient and worldwide concept, but he was the center of American transcendentalism.

Nature (1836): In this, his first book, Emerson asks, "Of what use is nature?"
- He begins at the most obvious point: nature is a commodity, it accommodates our practical needs.
- From there he moves toward ever more abstract uses—through beauty, language, discipline, and idealism, to spirit.
- Our intuitions about nature lead us steadily away from the impermanent and perishable toward the absolute. And as our relationship to nature becomes ever more spiritual, its evils disappear, displaced by goodness and virtue.

Essays: Since we are able to proceed without assistance directly to the truth of God, we can be self-reliant in all questions of conduct.
- In "Self-Reliance" (1841) Emerson tells us "Trust your emotion [intuition]…when the devout motions of the soul come yield to them heart and life." If this yielding is inconsistent with your past action ignore the inconsistency. "A foolish consistency is the hobgoblin of little minds." If refusal to conform offends society remember, "whoso would be a man must be a nonconformist."
- In "The Divinity School Address" (1838) Emerson urges his audience of prospective clergymen to "dare to love God without mediator or veil," not in conformity with the forms of the church, but self-reliantly.

- In "The American Scholar" (1837) he says, "Books are for the scholar's idle time," merely the record of what other men have thought. Through the power of self-reliant access to truth, originality should always be the aim.
- "The Poet" (1844) asks for poetry that finds its images in the American scene and poetry whose form is determined by what it is the poet wishes to say, not by traditional forms. Since nature corresponds exactly to mind, all truth preexists and all poems lie in nature already formed awaiting revelation by the poet.
- Related to this idea that nature reflects both God's mind and man's soul, men and women share a mystic unity "within which," Emerson says in "The Oversoul" (1841), "every man's particular being is contained and made one with all other," forming a basis for, among other things, a faith in democracy.

Method of composition: Difficulty in reading Emerson comes from his using the sentence as the unit of construction.
- Sentences are not logically linked but exist within the paragraph like "duck-shot held together by canvas" (Thomas Carlyle).
- Each repeats his idea in different terms. Sentence by sentence, paragraph by paragraph, he covers the same ground like a spiral that accelerates upward.
- He uses overstatement for its shock value, often at the beginning of an essay.

Poetry: Emerson believed that the poem should present concrete images that stand as symbols. In this he influenced Whitman, Dickinson, and modernist poetry generally.
- "Each and All" shows how the inextricable interdependence of all beautiful objects symbolize the perfect coherence of the cosmos.
- "The Problem" shows how the intelligence behind this cosmic wholeness discloses its purpose both in the beautiful unconscious forms of nature and in beautiful forms made by men complying unconsciously with the cosmic force.
- "Hamatreya" (Emerson was a student of Hindu thought) uses concrete imagery to convey the ancient theme that human pride passes but the earth abides.
- "Uriel" presents the insight that nowhere is there a straight line separating good and evil, right and wrong, connecting cause and effect, demarcating light and dark. These themes are present in "Brahma," a related poem.
- "Merlin" sets forth in ideal and heroic terms the role of the poet in society: to make plain to all the relationship between the real and the ideal.

Key 22 Margaret Fuller (1810–50)

OVERVIEW *Margaret Fuller was one of the outstanding figures in the transcendental movement, the able first editor of transcendentalism's primary periodical,* The Dial.

Career: She was a key figure in transcendentalism's work for educational reform. Her surviving writings establish her as a person of impressive intellect and a persuasive advocate of women's rights.
- Her principal book was *Woman in the Nineteenth Century* (1845).
- Moving from Boston to New York, she began a career in journalism that took her to Europe and into the midst of Italy's struggle for unification.
- Returning to America in 1850, she drowned when her ship was wrecked on the south shore of Long Island, New York.

Themes: Margaret Fuller argued in opposition to Emerson that women, like men, were inherently divine.
- Allied with this belief was her observation that no man was wholly masculine nor any woman completely feminine.
- Pessimistic about the likelihood of persuading men to her conviction, she declared that to improve their lives women must rely on themselves and on each other.
- She pointed out that the abolitionist fervor of the transcendentalists should logically lead them to urge the abolition of the bondage of women to men.

Key 23 Nathaniel Hawthorne
(1804–64)

OVERVIEW   *Nathaniel Hawthorne is ranked among the foremost of those writers of the middle of the nineteenth century whose work achieved that first maturation of American literature known as the American Renaissance.*

Works: He wrote well over a hundred stories, essays, and sketches, and four notable novels: *The Scarlet Letter* (1850), *The House of the Seven Gables* (1851), *The Blithedale Romance* (1852), and *The Marble Faun* (1860).

Narrative method: Hawthorne writes from a detached point of view in prose that approaches cool perfection.
- He consciously aims at carefully wrought and highly polished literary art in language elevated in diction, restrained in rhetoric, and gracefully economical.
- He uses a limited number of themes and character types in situations concerned with intricate moral problems whose resolution is often intentionally ambiguous.
- Allegory and symbol help disclose without didacticism Hawthorne's truth, which is psychological and universally human rather than religious or theological.

Themes: Hawthorne finds his materials in the New England Puritan past or in the heritage of Puritanism in a later day.
- The past, therefore, is a force living in the present.
- As we would expect from the deep Puritan concern with moral conduct, Hawthorne's work shows sin and its attendant guilt to be an inextricable part of life, and all men and women to share an inclination toward evil.
- If we yield to this inclination and conceal the deed, our secret guilt can destroy us. Our deed confessed and expiated, we can grow in virtue and find redemption.
- The unpardonable sin is the invasion of the sanctity of another person's soul, and through that invasion to bend the person to our will.

Stories and *The Scarlet Letter*: The student most often encounters in class those stories whose themes later appear in Hawthorne's greatest novel and universally praised classic, *The Scarlet Letter*.

- "Young Goodman Brown" leaves his newly married "Faith" to spend a night in the forest, Hawthorne's symbol for the abode of Satan. There he discovers—or dreams he discovers— the entire Puritan community, "Faith" among them, at devil-worship. He calls upon his "Faith" to refuse baptism into diabolism and awakens along a forest trail. He looks silently thereafter upon his Salem neighbors as secret and hypocritical sinners.
- In a parable less dark, the Reverend Mr. Hooper, from a sense of personal guilt unconfessed, dons for life a thin black veil, symbol of universal guilt concealed by hypocrisy. This emblem enhances his ministerial powers, just as a personal burden of guilt does for Arthur Dimmesdale in *The Scarlet Letter*, especially in counseling the sin-sick.
- Similarly, Hester Prynne's scarlet A gives her a sympathetic knowledge of sin in other hearts and makes her suspect that "if the truth were everywhere to be shown, a scarlet letter would blaze forth from many another bosom."
- But whereas Hester willingly acknowledges her guilt and therein finds salvation, Dimmesdale conceals his complicity in her shame and is destroyed as Roger Chillingworth coldly probes his heart.
- Chillingworth is thus guilty of the unpardonable sin and is the type of the morally irresponsible scientist foreshadowed by those other unpardonable sinners who destroy those upon whom they experiment—Dr. Rappaccini, Aylmer of "The Birth Mark," and Ethan Brand.
- For Hawthorne life was a grim business where even such a person as Robin's kinsman, Major Molineux, his head grown gray in honor, is brought down in disgrace by the vicious citizens of an infernal city where the seven deadly sins thrive and where Robin learns that he might rise in the world without the assistance of virtue.

Key 24   Longfellow, Whittier, Lowell, Holmes

OVERVIEW   *These New England poets lived their long lives wholly within the nineteenth century. The softening of religious orthodoxy had produced in them a sweet-tempered tone ranging from the melancholy of Longfellow to the gentle and genial satire of Holmes. They were widely read, admired, and even loved, but they were not originators. Their forms were well-worn and their subjects familiar. Although often platitudinous and sentimental, they showed that poetry could be competently written in America.*

Henry Wadsworth Longfellow (1807–82): He was the first American poet to live on his poetry.
- Not given to strenuous effort himself, Longfellow used the theme of perseverance in adversity in such popular poems as "A Psalm of Life" and "Excelsior."
- His awareness of the transience of experience accounts for the melancholy tone of "My Lost Youth," "The Fire of Driftwood," "The Jewish Cemetery at Newport," "The Tide Rises, the Tide Falls," and much else.
- "The Arsenal at Springfield" successfully likens the racked arms to a pipe organ to be played by "the death angel."
- He wrote three long narrative poems, *Evangeline* (1847), and at the height of his powers, *Hiawatha* (1855) and *The Courtship of Miles Standish* (1858). Despite their subjects, they lack specific American reference.

John Greenleaf Whittier (1807–92): Whittier was the only one of this group not of aristocratic birth and college education. His poems reflect his sturdy Quaker sense of human brotherhood ("Proem"), his abolitionist convictions ("Ichabod"), his pacifism (in tension with his abolitionism in "The Waiting"), and his rustic upbringing (in "Telling the Bees" and *Snow-Bound* [1866]). Despite his pacifism he was in support of the Civil War.

Oliver Wendell Holmes (1809–94): Among the "fireside poets," Holmes was the wittiest and most urbane. His vocation was medicine, poetry his avocation. His verse is mainly humorous, satirical but kindly.

- In "The Last Leaf" and "My Aunt" he has affectionate fun with the foibles of his ancestors.
- In "The Deacon's Masterpiece" he allows the reader to discover that the collapse of the superbly built "one-hoss shay" parallels the collapse of Jonathan Edwards' superbly built theology into irrelevancy to mid-nineteenth century society.
- Two poems are exceptions to the lightness of Holmes' work: "Old Ironsides," a ringing protest that saved the frigate *Constitution* from being scuttled, and "The Chambered Nautilus," where the chamber by chamber growth of the shellfish is a paradigm for spiritual growth.

James Russell Lowell (1819–91): Like Longfellow and Holmes, a professor at Harvard, cultivated, intelligent, Lowell was the least of the "fireside poets."

- Among his many long poems, only "The Cathedral" is readable today.
- In *The Biglow Papers* (1846 through 1848) Lowell protested the Mexican War in humorous dialect verse that hits the target again and again.
- In *A Fable for Critics* (1848) he caught the characteristics of principal American writers in critical vignettes that have stood up to time and delight us today.
- He was the first editor of the *Atlantic Monthly*.

Key 25 Edgar Allan Poe (1809–49)

OVERVIEW *Although he had little impact on poets immediately following him, the popularity he enjoyed in his day has endured.*

Influence: His use of symbolism strongly influenced the French and by reflection returned to America at the beginning of the twentieth century to help shape the literary movement known as modernism.

- Unlike his contemporaries, he was concerned only with beauty, not with morality. In this he anticipated the "art for art's sake" movement that came toward the end of his century.
- His "arabesque" tales drew upon the gothic tradition while those he called "grotesque" suggest northern European examples.
- He is the inventor of the detective story. His fictional devices for this genre have served writers ever since.
- As a critic, he was the first American to evaluate literary work by close analysis.

Creative method: Poe believed that long stories or poems lost their effectiveness in reader fatigue, and, indeed, that there was no such thing as a long poem. Consequently, almost everything he wrote was intended to be read at one sitting.

- In prose fiction he frequently aimed at creating a single effect coming at the climax and conclusion of the tale.
- Stories like "Ligeia," "The Fall of the House of Usher," "The Masque of the Red Death," and "Morella" end not with a completed human story, but with an intense shudder of emotion reached after a carefully prepared approach.
- His poems, too, often produce this "wow" at their end, as when the bereaved lover finds himself unexpectedly confronted in his forest walk by the tomb of "Ulalume," and the grieving young husband of "Annabelle Lee" lies down beside her corpse.
- Even when the death of a beautiful woman (his favorite theme) is not treated, as in "The City in the Sea," the poem ends with the annihilation of "that town" and all its dead but undecaying inhabitants.

Key 26 Henry David Thoreau
(1817–62)

OVERVIEW *Henry David Thoreau exemplified in his life and expressed in his work the characteristically American struggle for moral independence within a business society that prefers conformity. The books he wrote in his short life established him as a master of American prose and spread his influence throughout the world.*

Themes: The risk, while pursuing material goals, of missing what is most essential and rewarding in life; the pleasures of living near to nature and the hints such closeness gives of the divinity that lies behind nature's facts; the satisfactions of living life guided by self-discovered moral principles; on all questions of right and wrong— personal, social, and political— conscience must be the sole determinant; intuition provides the highest truths.

A Week on the Concord and Merrimac Rivers (1849): Thoreau structured this, his first book, on the days of the week, a chapter to each day. The pleasant narrative of a canoe trip carries the burden of transcendental thought as Thoreau looks behind his observations for their intimations of eternal truth.

"**Civil Disobedience**" (1849): Urges the citizen to refuse to cooperate with his government when its laws, policies, and actions are contrary to his conscience. The essay inspired both Mahatma Ghandi and Martin Luther King.

Walden, or Life in the Woods (1854): Thoreau's most important book. It is structured on the four seasons, beginning in summer and ending with spring. It offers Thoreau's answer to the question of how to subsist in nature while reserving most of one's time for observing, reflecting, reading, and writing—living, that is, in a direct and continuous relationship to nature and from its facts deriving ideal truth.

Key 27   Herman Melville (1819–1891)

OVERVIEW   *Moby Dick (1851) comes closer than any other book to being an American epic, yet its author, after an initial success with* Typee *(1846), was largely neglected in his lifetime. His reputation was not revived until the 1920s with the observance of his centennial and the 1924 publication of* Billy Budd, *left in manuscript at his death in 1891.*

Themes: Among the great variety of Melville's themes are:
- The preeminence of democracy as a basis for government
- The nobility of labor and the common man
- The necessity of preserving the traditional institutions of Western culture
- The ubiquity of evil
- The danger of merging the personality in the cosmic "all"
- The need to balance transcendental insight with empirical "truth"
- The hubris of seeking in nature ultimate answers to metaphysical questions
- The impossibility of man's returning to his original innocence, the pathos of life, the rapacity of the world

Narrative method: The style is elaborate, elevated, written with frequent rhetorical flourishes in a diction that is formal and highly literary. These characteristics, fatal in lesser hands, effectively serve Melville's intentions.
- He makes illuminating allusions to literature, history, theology, philosophy, and science.
- Almost all his work is in some degree symbolic and often suggests parable or allegory.
- His symbols are rich with significance, with a complexity and ambiguity that, when uncovered, provide both aesthetic and intellectual rewards.

Typee (1846): Fictionalized biography, the account of Melville's benevolent captivity by a tribe of pleasure-loving Marquesan "cannibals" and young Tommo's discovery that civilized man cannot return to paradise.

Moby Dick (1851): The common sailor "Ishmael" tells with realistic detail the story of his symbolic voyage on board a whaler.
- The *Pequod*, with its polyglot crew and its harpooneers representing the red, black, yellow, and brown races under the command of

Captain Ahab, is Melville's Ship of the World, bent on discovering in the white whale the nature of the ultimate force governing the cosmos.

- Ahab's mad presumption in this quest ends in catastrophe. Ahab and all but Ishmael drown, the *Pequod* sinks, and Moby Dick, symbol of nature creative, destructive, and inextinguishable, is victorious once again over man's hubris.

Billy Budd (1924): The story of the conflict between Billy Budd's Christ-like innocence and John Claggart's satanic "Natural Depravity," a conflict resolved with godlike Reason by Captain Vere.

- The crucifixion imagery surrounding Billy's execution on the cross of the mainmast makes clear that Billy's death is a "ransom sacrifice" necessary, as Melville would have it in his conservative old age, to save the institutions of Western civilization from the "red meteor" of Napoleonic conquest.

"Bartleby the Scrivener" (1853): Combines humor and pathos in a parable that shows the poor scrivener driven to the wall of despair by the iron necessities of his pathetic life. There, with provoking passivity and maddening non-compliance and finally with his death, he unwittingly teaches his complacent employer to embrace at last the great commandment to love his fellow man.

The Encantadas (1853): This series of sketches on the Galapagos Islands discovers the evil in man again and again. We are prepared for this by Melville's description of "The Isles at Large" as flame-blackened as if by a "penal conflagration" and inhabited by creatures whose dominant sound is the reptilian hiss, and by "The Rock Redondo" where birds increasingly piratical and murderous rise above their harmless feathered brothers in tiers that circle the world-like sphere.

"Benito Cereno" (1855): Based on a mutiny of the slaves on the Spanish slaver *Amistad*, it is a covert criticism of Emersonian optimism about the goodness of man, rich in irony.

- Genial, naive Captain Delano misinterprets the situation on board the *San Dominick* and never comes to understand that Babo's desperate deception arises from his enslavement and the enslavement of his fellow Africans.
- The slaver, Don Benito, is presented as goodness imposed upon by misfortune and the murderous Babo as the good servant whose apparent spaniel-like loyalty is characteristic of his race.
- Melville's criticism of Emersonian optimism is clear. Unfortunately, his attitude toward slavery and its associated evils is ambiguous.

Key 28   Walt Whitman (1819–92)

OVERVIEW   *Whitman celebrated America as the great democracy where each individual, over time, could evolve to spiritual perfection. Declaring the human body to be the equal of the soul and asserting the equality of men and women and of all races and conditions, he found his truth in the light that came directly from his soul, independently of rational analysis.*

Theory: Whitman's poetry reflects the theories of Ralph Waldo Emerson in that the verse:
- Emerges organically as the fruit of the poet's own growth.
- Derives its form (free verse) not from traditional meters but from "meter-making argument."
- Finds its material in the common, familiar, and everyday life of Americans everywhere.

Poetry: Virtually all of Whitman's poetry is in *Leaves of Grass*, published during his lifetime in nine successively larger, revised, and reorganized editions between 1855 and 1892. *Leaves of Grass* was self-published and severely criticized for sexual content and extensive free verse.

"Song of Myself": The longest (and among the best) of his poems, in which the poet's soul records in a succession of vignettes and reflective interludes the picturesque surface of America and its democratic values, including his conviction that all mankind is immortal and evolving over time (however great) toward perfection.

"When Lilacs Last in the Dooryard Bloom'd": His lament on the death of Abraham Lincoln, one of the greatest elegies in English.

"O Captian! My Captain": This poem also mourns Lincoln.

Key 29　Harriet Beecher Stowe
(1811–96)

OVERVIEW　*Although she was thereafter to write novels and local color stories of her native New England, Harriet Beecher Stowe's great achievement was her anti-slavery novel of 1852,* Uncle Tom's Cabin, *a book that inflamed the North and shook the conscience of the South.*

Influence: Selling 300,000 copies within a year of publication, the story of its principal characters—Uncle Tom, Eva St. Clare, Eliza, Topsy, and the villainous overseer, Simon Legree—provoked a passionate response that helped bring on the Civil War and became a permanent part of the American imagination.

Themes: The iniquity of slavery; the virtue of submission to God's will; the universality of human feelings, aspirations, intelligence, and abilities.

The novel and its method: The sale of Uncle Tom and Eliza's little son Harry from the Shelby's Kentucky plantation generates two plots that proceed in opposite geographical directions, north and south.

- The plots are linked from time to time by events that rejoin, after many years, the surviving characters in the safety of Canada.
- Undisguised appeals to the reader's emotions make such events as the death of little Eva St. Clare and of Uncle Tom extreme examples of sentimentality, while melodrama like Eliza's escape across the ice of the Ohio River appealed strongly to the contemporary taste.
- To enforce her moral lessons, the author now and again speaks directly to the reader.

Key 30   Frederick Douglass (1818–95)

OVERVIEW   *The* Narrative of the Life of Frederick Douglass, an American Slave, *published in 1845 when its author was only 27, tells his story from childhood until his escape to freedom at the age of 20, when, to avoid being retaken, he changed his name from Bailey to Douglass. He revised and extended his autobiography in 1855 with* My Bondage and My Freedom *and again in 1881 with* The Life and Times of Frederick Douglass.

Slave narratives: Douglass' books are examples of the so-called "slave narrative," many of which appeared in the nineteenth century and became in the 1840s a staple of abolitionist propaganda. Among their authors Douglass is preeminent both for his literary style and for his remarkable achievements as a freeman.

- The "slave narrative" divides itself naturally into a story of "before and after"—the "before" portion recounting the horrors of slavery, the "after," the opening out of life's opportunities in freedom.
- Douglass, when free, became a confidant of John Brown, a recruiter of black troops for the Union army, an agitator for a just and speedily applied policy of Reconstruction, an effective advocate for adoption of the Fifteenth Amendment, a spokesman against discrimination for economic, social, legal, or gender reasons, and for many years the successful editor of his own newspapers, *North Star* followed by *Frederick Douglass's Newspaper.*
- Thus Douglass' autobiographical narratives are also examples of the characteristically American tale of the self-made man.

Key 31   Humor of the frontier

OVERVIEW   *The humor of "the Southwestern Yarn-spinners" came into being in the 1820s with the Jacksonian era and ended with the Civil War. Its region was western Georgia, Alabama, Mississippi, Louisiana, eastern Arkansas, and eastern Texas. The influence of this Southern genre was strong, surviving most significantly in the work of Mark Twain and William Faulkner.*

The tales and their heroes: The tales of the principal humorists were eventually collected and published in book form, unified only by their subject matter and the ongoing presence of their comic heroes.
- They turn violence, cruelty, bumpkin horseplay, and a touch of sex into rough humor expressed in colloquial Southernese, phonetically rendered.
- The authors were usually well-educated, sometimes distinguished, professional men of the region who published yarns in newspapers or sporting journals to be read by other men in barber shops, or on trains and steamboats.
- Their protagonists can be traced to Davy Crockett, the gamecock of the wilderness, "half horse, half alligator," and the tall tales he and a few other men using his name wrote.

Georgia Scenes (1835): By Augustus Baldwin Longstreet, has its clay-eating Ransy Sniffles to provoke the action and then stand safely aside.

Some Adventures of Captain Simon Suggs (1845): Johnson Jones Hooper created a hero "late of the Tallapoosy Volunteers" whose motto, "it's good to be shifty in a new country" governs his roguish behavior.

Sut Lovingood's Yarns (1847–67): George Washington Harris gave us Sut, the most outrageous and violent of all pranksters, who follows with sniggers the progress of some enraged bees into the underclothes of Sicily Burns.

"The Big Bear of Arkansas" (1841): The best single tale, by Thomas Bangs Thorpe, whose "Big Bear" tells of an "unhuntable bear" who when his time comes allows himself to be killed. Faulkner's long story "The Bear" is indebted to Thorpe.

Theme 4 THE CONTINENTAL
NATION, 1865–1900

*T*he Civil War transformed the distinct regions into a nation dominated by Northern business and finance. New laws encouraged industry on a large scale. The growth of cities followed—New York, with a population of 3 million, was the second largest in the world—and such cities came to dominate American life. The rapid growth of railroads made the entire nation accessible. The intensified awareness of regional differences and geographical extent was met by regional writers and local colorists. The ideas of Charles Darwin and Herbert Spencer undermined the supernaturalistic basis of American morality. Realism and, later, naturalism were literary modes well suited to interpret a materialistic society. Against these modes, writers and readers who demanded that literature advance ideal values fought a long, ultimately losing, battle.

Key 32   Regional writing and local color

OVERVIEW   *The Civil War and the rapid extension of railroads that followed awakened a new interest among Americans in the regions and localities of their reunited nation. One manifestation of this new interest was the emergence of regional writing and local color.*

Distinction: The line between the two becomes distinct when *Huckleberry Finn* (regional writing) is compared to *Roughing It* (local color). Mark Twain wrote the former as an insider bred to the region. He wrote the latter as a tenderfoot in Colorado and Nevada who highlighted what struck him as picturesque in each new scene.

Realism: Both regional writing and local color are instances of literary realism insofar as the narratives are set in contemporary time, the speech (often in dialect) is that of the common people whose stories they tell, and the action is plausibly motivated.

Authors: Prominent among writers of regional literature and local color were Sarah Orne Jewett and Mary E. Wilkins Freeman in New England, Charles W. Chesnutt and Joel Chandler Harris in the mid-Atlantic South, and George Washington Cable and Kate Chopin in the deep South. Hamlin Garland wrote of rural life in the Midwest, and Bret Harte of the far West mining camps.

The work of Mark Twain, a major regional writer and local colorist, transcended the genres, as did that of Stephen Crane, whose local color tales of the West and Southwest are part of his larger achievement.

Key 33   Mark Twain (1835–1910)

OVERVIEW   *Samuel L. Clemens grew up in the river town of Hannibal, Missouri. For three years before the Civil War, he piloted a Mississippi steamboat and found on the river his pen name, "Mark Twain." Shortly after the outbreak of war he went west by stagecoach, finding literary gold on the mining frontiers of Nevada and California. Out of these experiences came work so rich in regional flavor and the spirit of the times that he has been called with justice our most American writer. The world delighted in his humor tempered by the pathos of his view of the human condition.*

Themes: The trustworthiness of the truths of the heart, the moral decline that accompanies growing up, the pleasures of rural childhood and the sense of loss when childhood is past, hypocrisy and pretense deflated by humor, a reverential attitude toward women, the impotence of religious teaching in the face of temptation, the iniquity of slavery.

Narrative method: The structure of the fiction is generally simple, the events given in chronological order and without multiple story lines.
- In the fictionalized reminiscences, events are often interrupted by anecdotes recalled from outside the chronological time frame.
- The style is colloquial, exact, and incisive, while remaining easy and lucid, giving a perfect sense of regional dialect through its diction and word order, avoiding on the whole the phonetic rendering of speech popular at the time.

Tom Sawyer (1876): Tells the melodramatic story of the boy Tom and his friends Huckleberry Finn and Joe Harper, who witness Injun Joe murder a fellow grave robber in a midnight cemetery. The consequences of their fear of Injun Joe, and their concern for the man unjustly accused of the crime cause further complications.
- The frustrated puppy love of Tom for Becky Thatcher and the prankish behavior of the three scamps leads to a frightening sequence in a miles-long unlighted cave in the Mississippi riverbank where Injun Joe, like Tom and Becky, is lost.
- Tom miraculously leads Becky to safety and claims her love, but Injun Joe, with $12,000 he has stolen, starves to death. Searchers find his body and the three boys share the treasure.

The Adventures of Huckleberry Finn (1885): Something of a sequel, it follows Huck, running from a depraved father, and Jim, a slave escaping from being sold down the river, as they raft south on the Mississippi current.

- The adventures of this picaresque pair involves them with thieves on a wrecked riverboat, the cold-blooded murder of a harmless drunkard, feuding planter families, and the schemes of two fugitive confidence men, the Duke and the Dauphin.
- The days and nights together on the river have fostered such love between the boy and the runaway slave that in a crisis of conscience, Huck renounces his Southern upbringing to continue helping Jim escape, thus assuring, as he thinks, his own damnation.
- In a dubious ending, Tom Sawyer's high jinks cannot spoil all that has gone before, and the book remains Mark Twain's masterpiece and a genuine piece of world literature.

Fictionalized autobiography:

- *Roughing It* (1872) is the account of Mark Twain's experience, considerably touched up, in Carson City and Virginia City, Nevada, during the 1860s. Mark Twain, the tenderfoot, gets comic fun out of his own ineptitude and ignorance, and sketches many colorful frontier types.
- *Life on the Mississippi* (1883) casts the cub pilot, Mark Twain, as an adolescent of about 16 (Twain was actually in his early 20s) and enhances the stature of his hero and instructor, the famous pilot Horace Bixby, by the comical presumption and irresponsibility of the cub.

Stories and novellas:

- "The Notorious Jumping Frog of Calaveras County" (1865) tells of a stranger to a California mining camp imposing on Jim Smiley, frog trainer extraordinary, by loading Jim's champion jumper with bird shot and winning the bet with a frog raw from the swamp.
- *The Man That Corrupted Hadleyburg* (1899) is the ingeniously plotted parable of a town proud of its reputation for honesty and of its motto, "Lead Us Not Into Temptation." However, when a stranger, wronged and vengeful, secretly and individually tempts its principal citizens, they yield to their dishonest greed for gold only to be publicly exposed. Learning from its humiliation, Hadleyburg adopts a new and undisclosed name and revises its motto to "Lead Us Into Temptation," seeking the vigorous moral exercise temptation brings.

Key 34   Emily Dickinson (1830–1886)

OVERVIEW   *Emily Dickinson was born in the western Massachusetts village of Amherst. Except for brief visits to Boston and to Washington, D. C. and a year at Mount Holyoke, she spent her life there, mainly within the grounds of the family mansion. Despite such limited experience she produced 1,775 poems, only seven of which (and these over her protest) were published during her lifetime. For the first two or three years of her career, she wrote nearly a poem a day, and altogether, she produced verse of such quality that she is placed with Walt Whitman in the first rank of nineteenth century American poets.*

Poetic method: She adapted to her purpose the structure of the Congregational hymns she was accustomed to singing, and hence her verse forms are simple and repetitious.
- Such is the pressure of her thought and the intensity of her emotion, however, that she frequently shatters syntax by cramming her expression into these tight stanzas. The punctuation is often idiosyncratic.
- The reader is thus forced from time to time to leap imaginatively with the poet across chasms of unexpressed meaning.
- Verse of such concentration, together with its wit and irony, anticipates the Modernist poets of the twentieth century.

Themes: Nature as a source of simple delight recurs as a theme in such poems as "I'll tell you how the sun rose" (J. 318), "A route of evanescence" (J. 1463) and "Bees are black with gilt surcingles" (J. 1405).
- Often, however, the theme of nature is given metaphysical implications as in "I taste a liquor never brewed" (J. 214), "Further in summer than the birds" (J. 1068), and "Of bronze and blaze the sky tonight" (J. 290).
- Such implications point to Dickinson's preoccupation with the themes of God, death, and immortality.
- In treating these latter themes Dickinson discloses deep anxiety—"There's a certain slant of light" (J. 258)— and on many occasions scepticism about the character of the orthodox God—"Safe in their alabaster chambers" (J. 216), and in such a poem as "The brain is wider than the sky" (J. 632), even God's existence.

Key 35 American literary realism

OVERVIEW *This genre which dominated American prose fiction from 1865 to 1900 is indebted to Balzac and Flaubert in France and to George Eliot in England. It departs from the sentimentality and idealization of life often characteristic of the Romantic novel that preceded it in its conscious desire to represent life in fiction with sincerity and honesty.*

In America: Generally speaking, American literary realism sets its story in the here-and-now and among persons of average social position, accurately reproducing their speech and manners in actions which are true to human behavior.
- The characters contend, on the whole optimistically, with ethical problems which they attempt to solve pragmatically and arrive at the end of their story without the help of coincidence or improbable intervention.

Authors: The foremost American realists were William Dean Howells (1837–1920), realism's most vocal proponent; Henry James (1843–1916), the greatest of the realists and often called "the father of the psychological novel"; Edith Wharton (1862–1937); and Ellen Glasgow (1874–1945). Mark Twain (1835–1910) is usually counted among the realists, although his fidelity in capturing the essence of a region and its people often departs from realism by presenting exaggerated characters in lurid action and improbable melodrama.

Key 36 William Dean Howells
(1837–1920)

OVERVIEW *Howells was a self-taught Ohioan who came East after the Civil War and succeeded, first in Boston and later in New York, in dominating the literary scene. He was the most vocal advocate of the new anti-Romantic realism which he defined as "the truthful treatment of materials," and called for fiction that was "true to the motives, the impulses, the principles that shape the lives of actual men and women." Prudish in the fastidious avoidance of sex in his 35 novels, he nonetheless vigorously championed young writers like Stephen Crane who were writing with a new candor.*

Themes: The essential goodness of the provincial American, the consequences of innocence unknowingly violating social taboos, commercial integrity in conflict with fraud and greed, the decay of morals in modern life, the struggle between the classes, the need for a democratically mandated social revolution.

Fictional method: Howells built his novels as a succession of dramatic episodes. His characters are shaped by what they say and do rather than by the revelation of what takes place in their consciousness.
- His generally well-shaped novels avoid the squalid, the lurid, and the violent.
- Actions are well-motivated and generally turn upon an ethical problem.
- Speech and manners accurately reflect middle class life of the day.

The Rise of Silas Lapham (1885): Usually called his best novel.
- The sturdy country-bred Lapham succeeds as a paint manufacturer and meets with an opportunity to rise steeply in Boston society.
- The overcommitment of his resources and the emergence of powerful business competition tempt him to take unethical though legal advantage in a deal made more tempting by the loss of his nearly completed Back Bay house to fire.
- His lack of experience makes his excursion into society a fiasco, but his integrity survives his commercial temptation.
- His fortunes fall, materially and socially, but he rises morally.

Cutting his losses in honest transactions he retires in modest comfort to his native Vermont farm.

"Editha" (1905): Editha Balcom, passionately aroused by the cause of the Cuban people, uses his love for her to persuade George Gearson to overcome his philosophical opposition and volunteer for the Spanish American War. He is killed in his first attack. When George's bitter mother denounces her as a romantic and destructive fool, Editha is emotionally confused until a friend, calling the mother's behavior "vulgar," lets Editha resume her self-idealizing posturing.

Criticism and Fiction (1890): His conception of American literary realism, arguing that fiction should find its materials in the commonplace, average, and everyday events of American middle-class life.

- He demanded that characters act from psychologically valid motivation and that the narrative proceed without resort to accident or coincidence.
- Avoiding the extremes of society and any indecency that might taint the purity of young women he asked novelists to concern themselves with "the more smiling aspects of life, which are the more American." Howells was indeed prudish and over-optimistic until late in life, but he wrote a number of very good novels that can be read with pleasure today and which give an accurate, if incomplete, picture of an era in American social history.

Key 37   Henry James (1843–1916)

OVERVIEW   *Through James, the novel in England and America reached a new level of maturity and refinement. From the beginning of his career he brought to the craft of the novelist a high seriousness and a new sense of the writer's responsibility for the integrity of his work. While he lived, no one in England or America wrote novels more worthy of admiration. His influence was strong on novelists as diverse as Joseph Conrad, Edith Wharton, Ernest Hemingway, and William Faulkner.*

Themes: Three themes are of principal importance:
- The international theme—American innocence, inexperience, and cultural ignorance confronted by European moral relativism, social sophistication, sense of tradition, and knowledge of a rich culture.
- The nature of art—the creative process and the artist's conflict with social convention, false values, and limited imagination.
- The individual in search of a richer life.

Narrative method: James' powerful imagination exhausts the possibilities of his fictional situations. The resulting narrative is jampacked with information, distinctions, shades of meaning, and so on.
- In his "late manner," this information is often conveyed in multiple dependent clauses that create elaborate sentences requiring close attention.
- He writes in long, solid blocks of narration, but even when the density of his prose is broken by a passage of dialogue, the conversation carries the story forward with the efficiency of an essay in logic.
- To enhance his realism, he tells his stories through the consciousness of a single character, never himself entering the story directly.
- His novels and tales are carefully built with an architecture in which all parts are carefully proportioned and balanced. In this matter of form he was superlatively a master.

Novels:
- In *The American* (1877) Christopher Newman, a 35-year-old self-made American millionaire renounces business and goes to Europe in search of cultivation and a wife of the highest quality. Beginning in ignorance he acquires a smattering of Europe's culture, but despite his wealth, his quick intelligence, and his tall good looks,

the pride of an ancient French family denies him the countess he has chosen to marry.

- More cultivated than Newman when she arrives in Europe but much younger and with far less human experience, Isabel Archer of *A Portrait of a Lady* (1881) also seeks self-fulfillment. But wealth from an unexpected bequest and naive self-reliance make her vulnerable to the scheming of the Europeanized, exquisitely refined American, Gilbert Osmond, and his discarded mistress. Marriage subjects Isabel to Osmond's cold tyranny but pride, a Puritan conscience, and a commitment to the welfare of a step-daughter determine her choice to endure the death in life her marriage has become.

Stories:
- The long story "Daisy Miller" (1879) tells of a young American beauty from a rich but ignorant family, traveling in Europe with her vulgar, stupid, but well-intentioned mother. Wholly innocent of any misconduct, her American independence and self-reliance clash with the social conventions of an American enclave in Rome and lead to her pathetic death from malaria, her love unrequited by the Europeanized American, Winterbourne.
- In "The Turn of the Screw" (1898), another long story, a young governess in a remote English manor house tells how her predecessor and the absent master's valet, while enjoying a sexual liaison, had corrupted the young orphaned brother and sister now in her charge. The lovers, prematurely dead, return as ghosts, relentlessly pursuing their young prey, forcing the young girl to be removed to London and her brother, "his little heart, dispossessed" of the devilish valet, Quint, to die of emotional stress.
- In another ghost story, "The Jolly Corner" (1908), the expatriate Spencer Brydon returns to New York after 23 years in Europe to confront in the vacant Fifth Avenue mansion of his birth the ghost of the vicious entrepreneur he might have been had he chosen to stay at home and seek money instead of a rich cultivation.
- The "Beast" of "The Beast in the Jungle" (1901) is the vague and unidentified threat Marcher is convinced lies along the path of his life, waiting to destroy him. For years he postpones his marriage until his fiancee sickens and dies. With her death Marcher comes to understand that the beast was the fear itself, that "what might happen" was the nonhappening of anything at all.
- "The Real Thing" (1892), the story of a painter who illustrates novels, sets forth James' theory that art, if it is to convey a sense of reality, fails if it merely copies "the real thing" and succeeds only when the imagination creates a persuasive illusion.

Key 38   American literary naturalism

OVERVIEW   *American literary naturalism developed out of literary realism and shares some of its characteristics. Like realism, it is neither futuristic nor historical, but places events in the present time of the writing. It aims at accurate reproduction of the speech, manners, and landscape of its world, and psychologically valid motivations.*

Sources: Unlike realism, however, literary naturalism is conscious of its philosophical foundations, drawing upon science and especially upon Darwinism for its view of humanity, and upon the immediately antecedent work in Europe of Emile Zola.

Philosophy: The human person is regarded as a highly developed animal existing no longer a little below the angels but rather a little above the other apes.

- Such a human animal is responsive to the forces of environment like any other, possessed of all the animal hungers, and aims above all at survival.
- It is limited by its genetic heritage, the accident of its moment in history, the place in society into which it is born, and the economic forces with which it must contend.
- The fittest survive in the life struggle, the less fit go down.
- Human existence is deterministic.
- Freedom of the will no longer exists, and with its disappearance ethical choice becomes an illusion.
- The ethical problem at the heart of the realistic novel is eliminated, and behavior, because determined, no longer can be judged in terms of good and evil, right and wrong.

Naturalistic Fiction: The illusion of ethical choice is strongest among the educated and the economically well-off. Therefore, the literary naturalist to demonstrate in fiction the validity of his theory looks for his characters among the underclasses of the cities, the rural poor, and because they have no buffer of civilization between themselves and raw nature, the primitive and the aboriginal.

- In the naturalist's world, metaphorically and sometimes literally "red in tooth and claw," violence replaces the decorum of the realistic novel and sex emerges from behind realism's taboos.
- Because it tells the stories of those helpless beneath the forces that bear upon them, the mood is pessimistic.

Key 39 Frank Norris (1870–1902)

OVERVIEW *Norris' fiction combines literary naturalism with an emphasis on unusual experience and passionate emotion that Norris defined as Romanticism. The subject matter broadened the range of what was permissible in the American novel of the day. The Octopus (1901), flawed by conceptual inconsistencies, is an epic of the far West, a notable attempt at "the great American novel."*

Themes: Nature as inextinguishable force: growth, sex, hunger, climate and environment; genetic determinism; economic force as natural law; evolutionary regression (atavism); the destructiveness of greed; pessimism in the short view of human existence, optimism in the long.

Fictional method: A conventional prose style that presents no difficulties for the reader builds the narrative by successive dramatic scenes. Norris observes his out-of-the-ordinary, often violent fictional world closely and accurately. His powerful imagination penetrates to the stormy emotional heart of his characters.

Novels:
- *McTeague* (1899) is the story of a hammer-fisted and unschooled San Francisco dentist and his young wife. An envious rival, fate, greed, and atavistic reversion to type in both husband and wife lead to his bludgeoning her to death and the lurid double death of McTeague and his rival, Marcus.
- *The Octopus* (1901) tells of the struggle between speculative California wheat ranchers and the railroad. The greed of both factions together with the inexorable operation of economic forces bring about tragic endings to the several intertwined narratives.

Stories:
- "A Deal in Wheat" (1902) tells of a wheat grower ruined by a manipulated commodities market and of the financiers to whom wheat is a game of money and power, of "chicanery and oblique 'shifty' deals."
- Chapter Nine of *Vandover and the Brute* (1914) tells of a passenger steamer wrecked off the California coast. Vandover's basic animality overwhelms his moral nature at the first violent moment of the grounding. Although soon afterwards he masters his instincts, he discovers how feeble the best efforts of captain, crew, and survivors are in their struggle with the violent sea.

Key 40 Stephen Crane (1871–1900)

OVERVIEW *In a brief career ended by his death at 28 from tuberculosis Stephen Crane produced a body of work that marks the point where American fiction broke with the British tradition. His characters live amidst violence, and Crane observes them with pessimistic detachment, accounting for their behavior with an instinctual understanding of psychoanalysis and social psychology well in advance of his day. Crane's world is governed by a God indifferent to the fate of mankind and unable to·intervene in human affairs.*

Themes: The effect of fear on behavior runs through all Crane's work and is seen in his treatment of war, of man's irrational responses to the conditions of life, of poverty and its associated vices, of unprovoked cruelty, and of the insignificance of our meaningless lives.

Narrative method: Crane's parallel career as a reporter accounts for the objectivity of his narration, for the accuracy of his observations, and for the unaltered sequence in time of his fictional events.
- The swift impressions he conveys reflect his journalistic feature-writing (such as his "Experiment in Misery") and the violence and chaos of the world he imagined is found in his frequent departure from normal syntax.
- Irony discloses the meaning in all his major work.

Novels:
- In *Maggie, A Girl of the Streets* (1893) Crane refutes the Social Darwinist conviction that the possession of moral qualities superior to the environmental norm enhances the likelihood of survival. Pretty Maggie Johnson hungers for beauty, order, and love, but her attempt to find these through Pete the bartender lead to her ruin and suicide. Equally ironical, if Pete had lacked a conscience, Maggie's death would not have sent him on a compulsive search for reassurance that he is "a good feller," a search that destroys him.
- The psychological masterpiece *The Red Badge of Courage* (1895), rich in irony, shows that Henry Fleming's fear accounts both for his "cowardly" flight and his "heroic" attack. Neither action has any effect on the outcome of the engagement, and Henry's complacency shows that his day ends not in self-understanding but in self-deception.

Stories:

- "The Open Boat" shows four survivors from a sunken gun-runner, captain, oiler, cook, and correspondent, representatives of mankind in the same boat together, rowing toward the Florida coast. The sea is not dangerous. Nature is indifferent, not hostile. The passage is arduous, the threat of death is present in each mind, and a sense of brotherhood grows among the castaways. When on the point of landing the little boat capsizes in the surf it is ironically the young and able oiler whose selfless quiet heroism is rewarded with death.
- In "The Bride Comes to Yellow Sky," town marshall Jack Potter arrives by train with his bride of a few hours to find Scratchy Wilson drunk and shooting up the town once again. Scratchy confronts the unarmed marshall in a showdown, but when the bride is introduced, dowdy and unattractive though she is, social convention tames all of Scratchy's ferocity and an era of violence comes to an end.
- "The Blue Hotel" shows how disastrous the consequences can be when we project our own conception of reality upon the world. The Swede, his mind apparently filled with tales of a wild West already passed into history, finds in a peaceful community the hostility, dishonesty, and violent death he created by his expectations.

Poems: Stephen Crane is considered a minor poet, but his idiosyncratic verse has a terrible intensity that expresses in concentrated form his view of the cosmos.
- God is cold to the man adrift on a slim spar, Crane pointing out that if God ever swerves from the mechanistic determinism of his creation to alter an event, the entire cosmos will decohere.
- When addressed by a man who declares, "Sir, I exist!" this cosmos replies, "However, .../ The fact has not created in me / A sense of obligation."

Key 41 Jack London (1876–1916)

OVERVIEW *Jack London was a highly talented writer, mainly self-educated, whose intellectual commitment to a classless society conflicted with his individualistic temperament, a conflict ended by his probable suicide at 40. He published 49 volumes, writing too fast and rarely revising, but his best work is of an enduring excellence.*

Sources: His literary naturalism followed from his reading such scientists as Darwin and Haeckel, the "scientific" philosophers Marx and Herbert Spencer, and Friedrich Nietzsche, whose transvaluation of values authorized "the will to power" and prophesied the superman.

Themes: Men and women are animals whose behavior is determined by the laws of nature, where the fittest thrive best and individual claims on life must be subordinated to the survival of the species.
- In order to survive in a changed environment, animals, including mankind, can regress from the level of behavior to which evolution has brought them to more primitive levels.
- Directly confronting nature, men and women can become equal partners in life's struggles, and women, with the requisite moral and physical strength, can fulfill themselves despite the genteel standards and restriction of the day.

Narrative method: London writes simply and chronologically in the vocabulary of common speech. The fiction, with few exceptions, is created from London's personal experience.

Novels:
- *The Call of the Wild* (1903) is the story of Buck, a dog taken to the Alaskan Klondike, where he must retrieve ancient instincts in order to survive. Buck answers the call of the wild and fights his way to the head of a wolf pack to stand at last howling at the arctic moon.
- In *White Fang* (1906) the process is reversed, and the little Alaskan pup, half wolf, half dog, undergoes the pain that accompanies his civilizing.
- *The Sea Wolf* (1904) gives us in Captain Wolf Larson, Jack London's version of the proto-superman. Larson subjects the effete Humphrey Van Weyden to an abusive but vitalizing education in seamanship and Nietzschean principles. Larson is killed at the end by the man he forced to discover his manhood.

Key 42   Native American writers

OVERVIEW   *Native Americans have produced a large quantity of poetry and prose. From prehistoric times until late in the nineteenth century, their literature existed only as an unwritten, anonymous oral tradition. Then anthropologists and linguists began the huge task of converting the tradition into a written literature that preserves the spirit of the original. Today Native Americans are writing poems and prose fiction that carry forward the creative work that reaches back in an unbroken line to its ancient beginnings.*

Themes: For the Native Americans, language was magical. They used it in songs, spells, and charms to control their world.
- Songs were chanted to make rain and to assure an abundant harvest, charms to cure sickness or alleviate pain, spells to overcome an enemy or win a reluctant lover.
- Language invoked the spirits of the sky, the earth, the winds.
- Their prose stories were short tales of their human origins, of their heroes or admired tricksters, of visitations by their gods, or of prophecy.
- Since language was held in high esteem, eloquence was a quality necessary for leadership.
- Until recent times, their only elevated language of recorded authorship was that of chieftains in negotiations with the white man, where resentment of betrayal, grief over the destruction of their culture, and the humiliation of defeat are sadly recurrent themes.

Theme 5 THE PROGRESSIVE ERA, 1900–1920

*T*he period from the 1890s to beyond the end of World War I was filled with enthusiasm for a wide variety of social and economic reforms. Most of the writers who wrote with sincere conviction were social critics. However, criticism did not always find a welcoming audience, and many authors found it difficult to publish what they wrote. To live, they turned to other occupations. Consequently, with notable exceptions like Edith Wharton, they spent years as part-time writers. Their work on farms, in law offices, in journalism, commerce, and construction interfered with the development of their technique and made self-cultivation difficult. On the other hand, their direct involvement in workaday America gave their writing a new spaciousness, rawness, sense of loneliness, and authenticity.

INDIVIDUAL KEYS IN THIS THEME	
43	Edgar Lee Masters
44	Edwin Arlington Robinson
45	Robert Frost
46	Carl Sandburg
47	Edith Wharton
48	Willa Cather
49	Theodore Dreiser
50	Sherwood Anderson

Key 43   Edgar Lee Masters (1868–1950)

OVERVIEW   *Masters is remembered for only one book,* Spoon River Anthology *(1915). In its day it was the most widely read book of American poetry, extravagantly admired for exposing Victorian hypocrisy and daring to show how sex rules human existence. Its more than 200 short poems weave the lives of some 243 Spoon River villagers into 19 narratives that make the* Anthology *read like a novel.*

Method: The poems are in free verse, the lines conveying a unit of thought. The words are those of conversational speech arranged with a somewhat greater concern for shapeliness than is common in prose. Masters' villagers speak one after the other from their graves their understanding of their lives illuminated by death.

Poems and themes: The dead disclose lives wasted by the narrow opportunities of a provincial village and maimed by hypocrisy, prudishness, sexual exploitation, ignorance, intolerance, and other kinds of moral ugliness. Each character speaks independently without comment from the author.
- "Petit the Poet" (his name suggesting smallness) now sees that in life he wasted his talent on conventional themes and worn out forms while neglecting the life around him and the beauties of the landscape.
- The sexual exploitation of "Elsa Wertman" is concealed for the sake of propriety, and she must remain the unacknowledged mother of a successful son.
- With the qualities of a pioneer, "Lucinda Matlock" has lived a life so long, productive, and satisfying that she admonishes her dissatisfied survivors, "It takes life to love Life!"
- The fully sexed "Margaret Fuller Slack" chooses matrimony over celibacy or unchastity only to find her literary talent sunk beneath unending maternity.
- In the shadow of his own death "The Village Atheist" reads the Upanishads and the Christian Gospels and struggles toward a glimpse of immortality somewhat as "Davis Matlock" recognizes that we should live with the zest of immortals, realizing that disbelief reduces God to physics and the afterlife to oblivion.

Key 44 Edwin Arlington Robinson (1869–1935)

OVERVIEW *Although he stands today among America's major poets, Robinson struggled for 25 years before wide recognition came to him in 1922 with the first of the three Pulitzer Prizes he would win. He is best known for his poems about the people who lived in the fictional New England "Tilbury Town."*

Form: Despite the essential newness of his poetry, he found traditional verse forms perfectly satisfactory for all he had to say throughout an immensely productive career, and he used them with admirable skill.

Poetic method: Whether in the vignettes of "Tilbury Town" or the book-length poems of his last creative phase Robinson aimed almost exclusively at creating characters and either hinted at or probed deeply their psychology.
- In the short poems he used the sonnet form, quatrains, or more intricate metric and stanzaic structures, always employing rhyme, and with an unfailing felicity.
- For longer poems such as "Ben Jonson Entertains a Man From Stratford," he wrote in a supple blank verse, the form he used for his Arthurian trilogy and his other book-length poems.
- He chose his words with care and frequently produced fine musical effects as when he describes Richard Cory as "imperially slim."

Themes: Life is agony, happiness but a wish.
- Through the darkness, however, we have faint intimations of light signifying we know not what.
- Fate is temperament as it was for Miniver Cheevy and Flammonde, making a successful life for them impossible.
- Fate can bring us to suicide as it does the woman of "Eros Turannos," the miller and the miller's wife in "The Mill."
- Richard Cory finds failure in success, one of Robinson's countless ironies, the reverse of Cliff Klingenhagen who finds if not success in failure, success at least in a muted life.
- Love can be rich and even ecstatic, but death parts even the happiest marriages and leaves a suicidal Luke Havergal, an inconsolable Reuben Bright, or the orphaned children over whom the young mother in "For a Dead Lady" bends so tenderly.

Key 45 Robert Frost (1874–1963)

OVERVIEW *Frost remains the most popular of twentieth century American poets. At the time of his death he was widely considered the most distinguished American poet. His narrative poems, the best yet written in our time, are realistic, dramatic, touched with wit and a quiet humor, and psychologically acute. His lyrical and meditative poems speak in the same colloquial New England voice as his narratives. Anyone can read the poems with pleasure, but each lyric is a metaphor where the more practiced reader finds a deeper satisfaction.*

Poetic method: Frost's pervasive irony allows him to raise philosophical questions without offering final answers, a reticence not often found in so socially and politically conservative a person.
- His reluctance to affirm or deny, however, provoked one poet-critic to call him "a spiritual drifter."
- This judgment, together with his rejection of Modernism, his exclusive use of old-fashioned verse forms, and his reliance on the subject matter of Romanticism (even though he uses it anti-romantically) has thus far kept him from a place in the front rank.
- Scoffing at free verse as "playing tennis without a net," Frost found traditional rhyme and meter along with blank verse the right forms for what he wanted to say.
- To the familiar forms he brought a distinctive voice, and by super-imposing his own cadences upon the regularity of the form, often created interesting rhythmic tensions.
- Although he found his syntax and diction in the common speech he heard in his rural New Hampshire, his poems are almost entirely free of countryisms.

Poems and themes:
- Nature does not respond to our love for her: the singing thrush ("Come In") is not inviting the poet to join it.
- And there is no certainty that ultimate knowledge, "heaven," is possible ("For Once, Then, Something") or even desirable ("Birches").
- The conditions of life declare our fallen state ("Nothing Gold Can Stay"; "The Oven Bird"), and we can know the terror of spiritual emptiness ("Desert Places"; "Acquainted With the Night"),

although salvation lies in the exercise of our imagination ("Directive").

- If there is a design for the Universe it is either diabolical or applicable only to the macrocosm ("Design").
- A choice that "made all the difference" in life ("The Road Not Taken") may have been made without strong preference or sufficient facts, but the consequences "ages and ages hence" probably will cause merely a sigh that we must live one life at a time.
- Such acquiescence in life includes a recognition that no matter how abundant the harvest ("After Apple-Picking"), we can have "enough of apple-picking" and, reading the signs of approaching death, accept our long sleep hardly troubled by a few unanswered metaphysical questions.
- Until then, however, life presents "promises to keep," to ourselves and others, and even at a suicidal moment, "easy wind and downy flake" must not entice us to forget that we are obliged to live before we die ("Stopping by Woods on a Snowy Evening").
- *Mending Wall* includes the famous line "Good fences make good neighbors." It comments sardonically on human relations.

Key 46   Carl Sandburg (1878–1967)

OVERVIEW   *Carl Sandburg wrote his "simple poems for simple people" in the words of men and women in big cities or on prairie farms, using the rhythms of their speech, the structure of the way they said things.*

Subjects: His poems celebrate work and the worker, men and women alike, and the strength, arrogance, coarseness, and vitality of a young nation. The title of his book-length poem, *The People, Yes* (1936), is a key to his subject matter and his populistic sympathies.

Poems and themes:
- In what is perhaps his best poem, "Chicago," he creates the myth of the city as a blue-collar worker, young, turbulent, vigorous, dynamic with the promise of productive growth.
- He uses irony to hold up for praise and sympathy the lives of ordinary men and women in contrast to their employers and their social and political leaders in such poems as "Southern Pacific," "Child of the Romans," and "A Fence."
- The theme of pain, anguish, pride, all human endeavor lost in time's oblivion is the ironic point of "Cool Tombs," "Grass," and "Four Preludes on Playthings of the Wind."
- Although Sandburg disclaimed any connection with the Imagist movement, such poems as "Fog," "Prairie Waters by Night," and "Nocturne in a Deserted Brickyard" have the concrete and objective qualities demanded by the Imagists.
- Sandburg's defects are a failure to convey distinct feeling or articulate lucid ideas, the result, apparently, of his being satisfied to write without the effort required for great art.

Key 47   Edith Wharton (1862–1937)

OVERVIEW   *Edith Wharton devoted her attention mainly to the struggles of individual members of exclusive societies to fulfill themselves within the rigid behavioral demands of their class. Born into wealth and privilege in New York City, she wrote as an insider principally of characters whose lives were patterned on those of New York's "four hundred" socially preeminent families. She was an excellent craftsman but the importance of her many books is limited by her conviction that "society" as an exclusive elite, in America and elsewhere, was indispensable to civilization.*

Narrative method: Edith Wharton's literary roots are in the nineteenth century. She was not an originator but followed the example of the writers most esteemed during her formative years. One of these was Henry James, and although it is inaccurate to speak of her as the "female Henry James," she wrote with Jamesian precision and with his control of the fictional point-of-view.

Themes: Hypocrisy stands behind the moral rigidity of "society," but despite its restrictive power, "society," in the narrow sense, is where life at its richest is to be experienced, an experience not to be enjoyed without plenty of money.
- Within society generally, sexual passions define interpersonal relationships and underlie the choices that determine the course of life.
- Like the other novelists within her tradition—James, Glasgow, and Cather among others—the driving force of sex is clearly but not explicitly presented.

Novels and stories:

The House of Mirth **(1905):** The tragic story of Lily Bart, wellborn but without money in a society where money is the only guarantee of security. Tempted to use her beauty to gain the support of a very rich man, she resists only to be abandoned by her weak lover to a life of moral drifting.

The Age of Innocence **(1920):** Perhaps her best novel, it pairs the charming but unhappily married Countess Olenska with a weak lover, Newland Archer, who, when the means of escape are provided, is too timid to leave the security of aristocratic New York society and follow her to Europe and their mutual salvation.

Ethan Frome (1911): Set in rural New England, it is a powerful short novel of illicit love, and the crippling, both physical and psychological, of Ethan Frome, who survives the accident that kills his young lover and becomes the object of his wife's lifelong vengeance.

"The Other Two": A deftly contrived tale of turn-of-the-century New York in which Waythorn, recently married to twice-divorced Alice, is amusingly maneuvered by circumstances into accepting his predecessors. Within the social niceties and gradations of aristocratic old New York, Waythorn, perfect representative of his class, comes in the end to accept "with a smile" the company of the genteel but socially inferior first husband, Haskett, and the wellborn Varick with his coarse streak, at afternoon tea with the serenely composed Alice.

"Roman Fever": Though published 30 years after "The Other Two" (1904), it seems more old-fashioned. From a restaurant terrace two rich New York widows, Alida Slade and Grace Ansley, look down upon a Roman vista. Beautiful Babs Ansley hurries by with a laughing Italian nobleman, and provoked by envy (her own daughter is unattractive) Mrs. Slade confesses to having forged 25 years earlier a letter from her fiance, Delfin Slade, proposing a love meeting with Grace Ansley in the dark Colosseum. Mrs. Slade taunts her friend with having been deceived and waiting alone in the dark, contracting the Roman Fever that removed her as a rival. Grace Ansley quietly reveals that she answered the forged letter and indeed met Delfin in the ancient ruin. Alida, conceding that defeat, derisively points out that for 25 years all her friend has had for consolation was a forged letter. The crushing irony is reserved for the final sentence: "I had Barbara," says Mrs. Ansley.

Key 48   Willa Cather (1873–1947)

OVERVIEW   *Willa Cather was one of the women novelists who came into prominence during the first years of the twentieth century. A regionalist and a realist, she describes the lives of immigrant farm people in Nebraska where she grew up in the late 1800s.*

Themes: Lives of immigrant pioneers, the effect of a harsh environment on character, the interaction of native and immigrant cultures, the history of Canada and the American Southwest, exploration versus cultivation, the artist versus society, materialism versus the spirit.

Method: Cather remained committed to the core principle of American literary realism: the truthful treatment of material. Her economically written ("unfurnished") novels do not depend on plot but chronicle the lives of men and women who live intensely and whose virtues outweigh defects. Her language reflects ordinary speech.

Novels: Two novels of immigrant families struggling to establish farms on the Nebraska prairie are *O Pioneers* (1913) and *My Antonia* (1918). *Death Comes for the Archbishop* (1927) is a fictionalized history of the mission of Father Latour among the peasants of New Mexico during the second half of the nineteenth century.

Novellas and stories:
- "Paul's Case" (1905) is the story of a boy whose sharp appetite for glamour is revolted by the tedium of high school and the squalor of his Pittsburgh home. Alienating all around him by his contempt, deprived by his father of his slender connections with a more brilliant world, he steals money enough for a week of high indulgence in New York. When punishment is near, he throws himself in front of a locomotive.
- Strong-willed Myra Driscoll, in *My Mortal Enemy* (1926), renounces wealth to marry Oswald Henshawe and leave the Midwest for New York to live the good life of cultivated society at the extremity of their means. After many years of not unmixed happiness, a flutter in Henshawe's world of finance reduces the couple to poverty. The brilliant, self-centered Myra, now in her 50s, sick in a cheap San Francisco hotel and attended by her devoted Oswald, is discovered by the novella's narrator, and we witness her last pathetic days, her vivid spirit still aflame.

Key 49 Theodore Dreiser (1871–1945)

OVERVIEW   *Dreiser, more than any other writer of his time, marked the break between the genteel idealism of the nineteenth century and the more direct and candid treatment of human experience of the twentieth. Widely criticized for a ponderous and awkward style, he must at last be acknowledged as a man of courage and integrity whose power and vision in fiction made him a novelist of broad influence and high achievement.*

Narrative method: His fiction was made of countless observations reported realistically in chronological sequence, detail piled upon detail to establish causation and motivation. Dreiser from time to time steps into his fiction to offer comments on character types and situations. Style was ignored in the pursuit of truth. Humor was entirely displaced by earnestness.

Themes: Men and women seek sexual gratification, beauty, and power, and achieve their desires to the degree determined by their talent, temperament, and place in society.
- Freedom of the will is an illusion and since "chemisms" drive us to triumph or failure, we merit neither praise nor condemnation. We act as we must.
- But life after all is an awesome mystery and mankind is to be regarded with profound pity.

Stories:
- In "The Second Choice," Shirley, daughter of a working class Chicago family, is pretty enough to enjoy a sexual relationship with the handsome Arthur but barely imaginative enough to respond to his view of life. When the prospect of adventure and material success calls self-centered Arthur away, the marginal Shirley, heartbroken, falls back on a dull but devoted railroad clerk, a "second choice" that is no choice at all but very close to necessity.
- The Theresa of "Old Rogaum and His Theresa" is a voluptuous 18-year-old living in turn-of-the-century New York over her immigrant father's lower east side butcher shop. The tenement neighborhood offers no way for the girl and her friends to satisfy their hunger for life other than the evening street and the forbidden company of young toughs. She is locked out when she flouts

once too often Rogaum's Old-World obsession with obedience, order, and propriety. She must be rescued at four in the morning from the precinct station, the threats to her virtue turned aside, in an ending where the tragedy is merely deferred.

- "Nigger Jeff" is about Elmer Davies, a young city reporter through whose eyes the rural action unfolds, and his discovery of the cost of violent crime in terror and grief not to the raped white farmer's daughter (she is barely mentioned) but to the lynched black farmer Jeff and his family. The story shows Dreiser's strong sense that we act from mysterious motives and that love and sympathy should supplant our inclination to judge and condemn.

Key 50   Sherwood Anderson
(1876–1941)

OVERVIEW   *Anderson was among the first in America to put Freudian psychology to literary use, to realize that men and women act upon impulses rising out of the unconscious and from experiences long overlaid by time.*

Achievements: Never a master of the novel, his achievement lies in the short story. For his best book, *Winesburg, Ohio* (1919), he gathered related stories into a loose unity where the sum became greater than its parts. Courageous in treating sex as central to behavior, Anderson influenced the generation of American writers who emerged just after World War I.

Themes: Bewilderment at the discontinuity between our inner and outer lives; the distortions of personality caused by frustrated desires; the existence in almost everyone of a grotesque, obsessive conviction; the spiritually blighting effect of modern industrial society; our drive toward self-actualization and a better life.

Narrative method: Anderson poses as an oral storyteller whose tales are spontaneous and unpremeditated.
- The reader feels that presence in the intentionally hesitant and groping manner that often color the telling, in the simple vocabulary, and in the conversational sentences.
- In a typical story, the central character relieves growing emotional pressure by an act of violence which discloses the meaning.

Stories:
- In "Mother"," Elizabeth Willard wants her son, George, to live for the romance, truth, beauty, and creativity she had once aspired to. Warped by her years in the shabby Winesburg hotel run by her failure of a husband, she imagines murdering him to prevent his imposing on his son a commercial career. Her vision recedes when George tells her he has rejected his father's values and wants vaguely "to go away and look at people and think."
- "Adventure" tells of Alice Hindman, seduced and left behind in Winesburg by an ambitious lover who intends to return for her but who, caught up in the attractions of Chicago, gradually abandons her. Years of waiting end when, naked in the rain, she offers herself to an old man stumbling home past her house in the

dark—drunk, deaf, and uncomprehending. She escapes to her room "to face bravely the fact that many people must live and die alone, even in Winesburg."

- In "Queer," Elmer Cowley has become estranged from the life of Winesburg by clerking for his eccentric father in a store "that sold everything and nothing" and was laughed at by all. Determined to leave town, he chokes in an attempt to explain his plans to the young *Winesburg Eagle* reporter, George Willard, and in his frenzy falls to beating him, reflecting later, "I guess I showed him I ain't so queer."

- The story title, "I Want to Know Why," is the anguished question asked by a boy, passionate about the splendors of thoroughbred racing, who discovers corruption in the trainer he thought shared his ideals.

Theme 6 AMERICAN LITERATURE IN THE MAINSTREAM OF WESTERN CULTURE, 1920–1945

*A*fter World War I, military, political, and business forces created a reactionary climate hostile to new social and artistic ideas. Many young writers left America for Europe, where they found freedom to scrutinize the values of their country more critically than had the older writers who were left behind. They also discovered new standards of craftsmanship and new techniques originated by an older generation of artists and thinkers—the French *symboliste* poets along with Yeats and Pound; novelists Proust, Joyce, and Gertrude Stein; cubism, post-impressionism, and dada in the visual arts; and the concepts of Freud and Einstein. But if their technical refinement was European, their subject matter was American, presented in American terms without timidity, shocking the genteel.

INDIVIDUAL KEYS IN THIS THEME

51	Modernism
52	Gertrude Stein
53	Ezra Pound
54	H. D. (Hilda Doolittle)
55	T. S. Eliot
56	Eugene O'Neill
57	Wallace Stevens
58	William Carlos Williams
59	Marianne Moore
60	Zora Neale Hurston
61	E. E. Cummings
62	John Dos Passos
63	F. Scott Fitzgerald
64	William Faulkner
65	Ernest Hemingway
66	Hart Crane
67	Thomas Wolfe
68	Langston Hughes
69	John Steinbeck
70	Richard Wright

Key 51 Modernism

OVERVIEW *Modernism is the term applied to an international movement dominating the arts of Western culture from shortly after the turn of the century until around 1950. In general, Modernism discloses a rejection of tradition and a hostile attitude toward the immediate past.*

Experimentalism: The "tradition of the new" was Experimentalism. There was a movement away from the warmly human characteristics of Romanticism (and in literature of Naturalism). At the same time a more analytical interest in personality led to an attempt to express the irrational workings of the unconscious mind both in painting (e.g., de Chirico and Dali) and literature (e.g., Joyce and Stein) and to stream of consciousness for presenting character.

Cultural relativism: Characteristic, as (for example) in African elements in Picasso's painting and in the anthropology of Eliot.

Myth: A structural principle of "The Waste Land," Pound's *The Cantos*, Joyce's *Ulysses*, and of other Modernist works.

Style: In poetry there was a broad dependence on the image and an insistence on spareness and precision in language.

Authors: In literature prominent Modernists were T. S. Eliot, Ezra Pound, Gertrude Stein, James Joyce, Virginia Woolf, William Butler Yeats, and Joseph Conrad.

Key 52   Gertrude Stein (1874–1946)

OVERVIEW   *Although most of her writing remains at best difficult for the common reader, the influence of Gertrude Stein on American writing in this century was exceeded only by that of Ezra Pound. An expatriate in Paris from 1903 until her death, she presided over a salon that attracted the avant garde and encouraged Modernism in all the arts. Her taste as a collector helped bring to the fore such giants as Cezanne, Matisse, and Picasso.*

Themes: The immigrant in urban America; the process of Americanization; the social dynamics of black urban society; lesbian experience; temperament as the unswerving determinant of behavior; biography and autobiography; the absurd (she has been called "The Mama of Dada"); women as independent, self-realizing persons.

Method: Using the sentence as her unit of organization; using simple words grammatically but in unusual arrangements; recreating the intensity of experience by maintaining a "continuous" or "prolonged" present through repetition ("beginning again and again"); conveying emotional states and essences of characters and objects rather than their physical qualities; disguising the lesbian content of sketches and poems through puns, *double entendres*, and suggestive imagery.

Writings:
- *Three Lives* (1909) tells the easy-to-read stories of three young urban women: two German immigrant serving girls, the managing Anna and the docile Lena, and Melanctha, a black girl who learns about life and love as she "wanders."
- In 1933 Gertrude Stein published her memoirs of the middle Paris years as *The Autobiography of Alice B. Toklas*. In clear prose, pretending that her lesbian lover is the author, Stein distances herself a little from the artists and writers she recalls during those magnificent Paris years.
- Characteristic of Stein when difficult, *Tender Buttons* (1914) offers "poems"—sentences, short paragraphs that juxtapose surrealistically unrelated images or use rational syntax in irrational descriptions of objects from the real world.

Key 53   Ezra Pound (1885–1972)
and the New Poetry

OVERVIEW   *Pound was a genius whose eccentricity verged on madness. Seen in perspective, nevertheless, his was the richest and most complex poetic life of this century.*

Career: Selfless in advancing the careers of artists he found worthy, a leader of modern literary movements, a translator of high distinction, and a poet of enormous achievement, his political and economic obsessions led him into anti-Semitism and treason, and to hospitalization as criminally insane. He declined after his release into penitential dejection and silence.

Creative method: Pound saw it as his task to explore from its beginnings the culture of the world, to retrieve the best that had been done, and to display that best in such a way as to "make it new."

- His translations from the Latin, the Anglo-Saxon, the Provencal, the ancient Chinese, and the Japanese are free recastings of the originals aimed at preserving the poetry that often is obscured by literal rendition.
- His Imagism demanded a new poetry that would be objective, adjective-free, lean, and hard, in which the image was to present an emotional and intellectual complex in an instant of time.
- Imagism evolved into the more active Vorticism where the vortex was a concentration of ideas in rapid movement. One such vortex was the *Metamorphoses* of the Roman poet Ovid, who made new for his time the legends of the gods Pound in *The Cantos* made new for the twentieth century reader.
- He, along with T. S. Eliot, developed the allusive method, a device characteristic of Modernism, whereby a poem is made more concentrated through allusions to antecedent entities within our culture. For the method to be successful, the reader must recognize the allusions.

Major poems and themes: Seeking a freer creative environment, Pound left London for Paris in 1920.

- In leaving, he criticized England in his first major poem, "Hugh Selwyn Mauberley" (1920), whose principal theme is the plight of the minor artist in England's commercial civilization. With the poem, Pound shed that part of himself represented by the over-refined, hyperaesthetic Mauberley, and turned his attention to

The Cantos, three of which he had published in 1917 and which, eventually reaching the number of 117, would occupy him for the rest of his life.

- *The Cantos* is a vast epic in free verse related by personae, including that of the voyaging Odysseus, whose identities Pound assumes. A few of its many themes are

  1. the possibility of experiencing the divine in nature through the poetic imagination,
  2. the need for a "clean" economy (its opposite signified by usura) if culture is not to die,
  3. the desirability of order, tradition, authority, hierarchy in society,
  4. the detestation of war.

Key 54   H. D. (Hilda Doolittle)
(1886–1961)

OVERVIEW   *H. D., as she signed herself, was an instinctive feminist who lived a liberated life. Her poetry provides the best examples of the principles of Imagism. That poetic movement of the years just preceding and following World War I insisted that poetry be direct, clear, and spare. The image was to create in a moment of time both emotion and idea. She did not confine her later poetry within these limitations. Her literary position is being re-evaluated and its early lustre being enhanced.*

Method: Short lines in free verse; economical language free of abstraction and generality; adjectives kept to a minimum. Freudian images often encode personal references.

Themes: Anguish, despair, fragmentation of the personality; the psychic plight of women; the beauty of nature; classical mythology.

Poems:
- "Oread" is the cry of a mountain nymph to the sea (imaged as a fluid forest) asking to be splashed violently and covered by its waves, pointed and phallic.
- "Leda" retells the myth of Leda possessed by Zeus with analogical images of a wild red swan beneath whose breast the water lily "outspreads and rests."
- In "At Baia" the speaker, whose love is unrequited or unconsummated, asks her lover for a dream-gift of vulva-like orchids, "piled in a great [Freudian] sheath."
- In "Helen" the poet muses on history to assert that resentful Greece could have loved Helen of Troy (with whom H. D. felt an identity) only if she were "white ash amid funereal cypresses."

Novel: Among her several novels, contemporary interest is highest in *Hermione* for its treatment of the psychic stresses felt by a woman in love simultaneously with a man and another woman.

Key 55   T. S. Eliot (1888–1965)

OVERVIEW   *From the end of World War I to the end of World War II Eliot was the dominant figure in both poetry and criticism.*

Career: "The Waste Land" in 1922 defined the post-war era as a despiritualized desert, an outlook adopted by most contemporary writers.

- In 1920 Eliot in "Tradition and the Individual Talent" set forth the theoretical basis for his own practice and by directing attention away from the personality of the poet to the poem itself prepared the way for the "New Criticism" to rule opinion in the 1930s and '40s.
- During these years Eliot, declaring himself "classicist in literature, royalist in politics, and Anglo-Catholic in religion," continued to produce poetry, criticism, and verse drama of high excellence.
- Three popular plays in verse were to follow, but with "Little Gidding" (1942), the last of *Four Quartets* (1943) begun with "Burnt Norton" (1935), his career as a lyric poet ended on the peak of his achievement.

Poetic method: Although never counted among the Imagists, Eliot joined Ezra Pound in his contempt for the looseness of much of the poetry appearing before World War I and strove to write verse that was direct, lean, adjective-free, hard, and objective. The French poet Theophile Gautier provided the model for this bare-stripped verse and from two other French poets, Charles Beaudelaire and Jules Laforgue, Eliot learned how to make poetry out of sordid urban life.

"The Love Song of J. Alfred Prufrock" (1917): Prufrock leads the reader past "one-night cheap hotels / And sawdust restaurants with oyster shells" to rooms where the women talk of Michelangelo and to "an overwhelming question" dropped on his plate by "hands that lift."

- There Prufrock, excruciatingly self-conscious and aware of his absence of purpose, loss of faith, of confidence, of will, fails to bring either himself or his auditor to confront the question, which is both spiritual and sexual.
- He ends his love song by submitting to rejection, renouncing even the dream of ecstasy, and acquiescing in living a submerged life.
- The reader encounters allusions to scripture, secular literature, and great figures out of history, allusions that generally belittle the triviality of the present by comparison with the glories of the

past. This allusive method, a fixture in the poetry of Eliot and of Ezra Pound, contributes heavily to the difficulty of the verse, a difficulty considerably abated by the footnotes in modern textbooks.

"The Waste Land" (1922): The allusive method is used with characteristic effect throughout "The Waste Land" to achieve enormous signification with relatively few words. The core allusion of the poem is to the Grail Legend of the Fisher King (himself an allusion to Christ) and to the infertile land over which he reigns.
- Spiritual infertility, not unconnected with sexual debility, is the core theme.
- By allusion Eliot evokes the ancient religions and fertility gods that lie behind the Grail Legend, and as all of the women in the poem merge, so too does mankind's age-old preoccupation with fertility, death, and resurrection merge all religions into one.
- Today we live within an apocalyptic nightmare of "falling towers / Jerusalem Athens Alexandria / Vienna London / Unreal."
- The poem's five divisions dramatize the plight of modern civilization.
- The consciousness that binds the five is that of the ancient prophet Tiresias, who "foresuffered all," and who as the poem ends merges with the Fisher King and with the poet, shoring up "these fragments" of our culture (alluded to within the poem) as a bulwark against chaos.

Early poems: "The Waste Land" was preceded by "Gerontion" (1920), whose speaker, a little old man representing our expiring civilization, is "waiting for rain," and was followed by "The Hollow Men" (1925) who live in a "dead land," a "cactus land" and upon whose every faintly felt impulse to live "Falls the Shadow" of paralyzing spiritual dryness. If these successive poems (including "Prufrock") express the poet's anguished search for spiritual vitality an advance would seem to be made when one of the wise men in "The Journey of the Magi" reports that finding the Christ child at Bethlehem "was (you may say) satisfactory." In witnessing that birth they found that they died to this world and were reborn to the world of spirit: "I should be glad," says the speaker of the poem, "of another death."

Religious poetry: In 1927 Eliot became a convert to Anglo-Catholicism (Church of England) and for the next three years was engaged in the writing of the poem that most directly describes his struggle toward Christian faith, "Ash Wednesday" (1930).
- The poem ends with the most minimal of affirmations, but by the end of *Four Quartets*, and in the additional light of two success-

fully produced verse dramas, *Murder in the Cathedral* (1935) and *The Family Reunion* (1939), affirmation would appear to be complete and unreserved.

- "Burnt Norton" (1935) lacks specific Christian content, but is concerned, nonetheless, with three kinds of time: 1. chronological time, 2. God's "time" or eternity, and 3. that "time" where "what might have been" remains still potential within God. In this scheme, the advent of Christ occurred at an intersection of time 1 and time 2. The poet's imagination can create in time 3 the mystical moment "that might have been" and experience the divine love he rejected in time 1, and be moved to cry out, "ridiculous the waste sad time / Stretching before and after."

- In "Little Gidding" (1942) Eliot assembles the leading symbols of all *Four Quartets* with their dominant themes of poetry, time and history, personal and temporal redemption, and the divine love that might have been and always is, and finds that our suffering and God's love are the same, that "the fire and the rose are one."

Key 56   Eugene O'Neill (1888–1953)

OVERVIEW   *Before Eugene O'Neill arrived, American drama was of minor significance and dramatists were thought to practice a trade, not an art. Then in 1915 O'Neill joined the just-formed Provincetown Playhouse, which scorned commercial theater and was open to O'Neill's experimentation. By 1925 he had won an audience for serious drama and opened the way for other American playwrights and theater groups. In the course of a long and prolific career, O'Neill won four Pulitzers, gained international acclaim, and in 1936 won the Nobel Prize.*

Dramatic method: Influenced both by the realism of Ibsen and the expressionism of Strindberg, the often poetic, romantic, and melodramatic O'Neill was in his time thought of as a realist, mainly because his plays had tragic implications. In the scripts, he gave unusually extended and explicit directions for their staging.
- His experiments in expressionism called for sets and performances distorting reality to intensify emotion and heighten symbolism.
- In the *Mourning Becomes Electra* trilogy he universalized the conflicts in a nineteenth century American family by superimposing them on the *Oresteia* of Sophocles.
- Elsewhere, he fitted his actors with masks and utilized the device of the Greek chorus.
- The autobiographical plays with which he ended his career show a spare and unelaborated realism.

Themes: The felt need to justify one's existence; the desire to ally oneself with some larger purpose; the persistence of racial memories; the need for a sustaining illusion; the destructive consequences of abusing alcohol and drugs; the Oedipal triangle; the eternally tragic predicament of mankind.

Plays:
- Yank Smith in *The Hairy Ape* is a fiercely proud stoker on an ocean liner who perceives himself to be at the heart of twentieth century speed and power. When an industrialist's daughter sees Yank instead as a hairy ape, the illusion that sustains him is shattered, and he declines to where he perceives himself as an animal and finds his death in the embrace of a gorilla.

- The one-act *Hughie* dramatizes in a virtual monologue by Erie Smith the way his illusion of himself as Broadway wiseguy, high-roller, seducer of Follies girls, and racetrack insider have held him together in a life of degradation, frequent humiliation, and only rare success.
- *Long Day's Journey Into Night* (1940) is O'Neill's masterpiece. The play is candid autobiography in which the Tyrone family is the O'Neill family thinly disguised. They are fogbound, the fog symbolic of their mutual alienation, inability to communicate, and their isolation as a family and as individuals. Whiskey and morphine encourage self-revelation, but what is revealed is revealed to the audience: the mother's guilt for refusing her familial responsibilities, the father's despair for the actor he might have been, the older brother whose dissolute life has been a reaction to his mother's hatred, the younger brother whom the older has tried to corrupt and who can find a kind of peace only by moving into the fog.

Key 57   Wallace Stevens (1879–1955)

OVERVIEW   *Stevens was a successful man of business who in 1923 at the late age of 44 published his first volume of poems,* Harmonium. *He stands today with Pound, Eliot, and William Carlos Williams as one of the greatest of modern American poets.*

Poetic method: Never much influenced by the literary movements of the day, Stevens' poems were unfashionably metaphorical and abstract.

- In *Harmonium,* especially, he departed from contemporary practice by using highly colorful and exotic diction, fanciful and gaudy imagery, wit, and droll comedy.
- His verse forms are conservative, mixing rhymed and unrhymed lines in rhythms basically regular.
- Many poems are in blank verse, but more are in a variety of stanzaic forms.
- Each stanza of "Thirteen Ways of Looking at a Blackbird" resembles the Japanese *Haiku.*
- From the beginning, but more strikingly as time went on, the poems are meditations.
- Some important poems, such as "Sunday Morning," "Peter Quince at the Clavier," "Le Monocle de Mon Oncle," and "The Idea of Order at Key West" are dramatic monologues.

Themes: The world is not arranged for our happiness, but since happiness is "the great subject" his poems imaginatively rearrange our physical world to bring it closer to our heart's desire: "Things as they are / Are changed on the blue guitar" of the imagination ("The Man With the Blue Guitar").

- In "Anecdote of the Jar," a simple work of art set in its midst rearranges "the slovenly wilderness" in response to our passion for order. For the girl in "The Idea of Order at Key West" "there never was a world for her / Except the one she sang, and, singing, made." Thus, for Stevens, order in our world is created by the imagination.
- And as "Sunday Morning" declares, over the ages our imagination has created and should continue to create new gods to meet the needs of our evolving consciousness.
- "Death is the mother of beauty" ("Sunday Morning"): knowledge that some day we will die intensifies the passing moment of

beauty, and since "Beauty is momentary in the mind" ("Peter Quince at the Clavier") we are moved to make it permanent in art. Therefore, "In the flesh it is immortal," since beauty created by Michelangelo, Shakespeare, or Beethoven lives only in those who experience it today.

- Life contains all we will ever know of heaven or hell, and for this reason "The greatest poverty is not to live / In a physical world," ("Esthetique du Mal").

Key 58 William Carlos Williams (1883–1963)

OVERVIEW *Like Walt Whitman, Williams was a poet of the everyday, the common, the contemporary, the near at hand. Because he was not a Modernist like Pound and Eliot, he was undervalued in the 1920s and '30s. However, by 1951, when Book IV of his epic,* Paterson, *appeared, he had come to be seen as a major poet. Young poets admired him and adapted their practice to his.*

Themes: The nature of poetry, the emergence of life, unfortunate humanity in its many guises, community history, sex and the erotic, nature, the richness of commonplace experience, the realities of industrial America.

Method: Avoided conventional or traditional forms; tried to report a thing or event with the intensity of the moment of perception, often composing spontaneously; scaled down his effects, believing that "less is more"; aimed at reproducing the rhythms of American speech and the words of the common man; avoided argument: "No ideas except in things."

Poems:
- "The Young Housewife" is "a fallen leaf" and the tires of the poet's car passing "rush with a crackling sound," suggesting the lack of juice in her humdrum life.
- "Tract" is a mock-angry denunciation of the artificialities of our funeral rites (and by implication of our poetry), calling for the replacement of all formalities with the rough, the ready-to-hand, the sincere and honest.
- "Portrait of a Lady," with its ironic reference to Henry James' Isabel Archer, is an exuberant celebration of the lady's beauty, freshness, erotic lure, and a delicate confession of the manner of his recent sexual connection with her.
- "Spring and All" applauds the will of bushes, weeds, vines to reawaken "naked, / cold, uncertain" into "sluggish, dazed spring."
- "The Red Wheelbarrow" is pure Imagism with a suggestion that the quality of our lives depends on the emotion with which we respond to such a picture.
- "This Is Just to Say" offers a loving, sheepish apology for a small

act of self-indulgence, sharply evoking the delight of eating those plums, "so sweet / and so cold."

- "Sunday in the Park," from Book II of *Paterson* (1948), shows "Dr. Paterson" (William Carlos Williams, M.D.) like a less flamboyant Walt Whitman, merging silently but happily into a succession of human scenes on a city park Sunday.

Key 59 Marianne Moore (1887–1972)

OVERVIEW *Marianne Moore was Modernist in technique but old-fashioned in morality. Pound, Eliot, and Stevens admired her irony and wit, the lean, dry, language in which she achieved exactness in description. But her values though admirable were uncomplicated, her ideas familiar, her temperament optimistic. Her great distinction lay in the strong visual effect of her poems, their detailed and quirky revelation of unexpected beauty and interest in the physical world.*

Themes: Animals (harmless and often exotic) used as in fables to present moral types in contrast to human behavior; writing, writers and the literary world; worthy causes; direct versus formalized representation of objects and events.

Method: American colloquial diction used in free verse that is often intentionally prosey; rhyme subtly, unobtrusively distributed; quotations introduced for the precision with which they say what the poet wants said; words cut to achieve tight expression (creating difficulties for the reader); faithfulness to the principles of Imagism.

Poems:
- "Poetry" haughtily rejects poetry as "all this fiddle," accepting as "genuine" only poetry that places in imaginary settings objects so accurately perceived and presented as to appear "real."
- "In the Days of Prismatic Color" distinguishes between the primeval, clear, unelaborated, self-evident truth of things and the overly sophisticated presentation of it, trendy and voguish, that, like a wave, passes into oblivion.
- "The Pangolin" describes in beautiful detail this creature astonishingly adapted to its mode of life. In contrast, Man, combining the abilities of many other animals, is fallible even in his crowning capacities (like writing) and full of contradictions. He is, nevertheless, unique in possessing a sense of humor, the impulse to strive upward—and the capacity to create art.

Key 60   Zora Neale Hurston (1891–1960)

OVERVIEW   *Although an important Harlem Renaissance writer, Zora Neale Hurston spent her first and last years in the black central Florida community of Etonville. Etonville gave her materials for her most important fiction, including her masterpiece,* Their Eyes Were Watching God *(1937).*

Themes: Selfhood and the African-American woman; African-American folkways and speech; the universality of the human experience; the dignity and order of African-American communities.

Method: Much of her fiction follows the patterns and diction of regional colloquial speech. The speaking voice dominates. One of her devices is the incomplete sentence added, sometimes in a short series, to modify or elaborate as in conversation a preceding full sentence. Spoken passages, often in superbly rendered dialect, are effectively followed without transition by passages in the third person that meditate in carefully literary language upon the fictional situation.

Fiction:
- *The Eatonville Anthology* (1927) creates—with anecdotes seemingly plucked from the memory at random and told with a soft smile—the portrait of an autonomous black town in the early twentieth century.
- *Their Eyes Were Watching God* (1937) is the story of the search by a young black woman for self-knowledge and self-fulfillment. This excellent novel of the black experience carries the ring of absolute sincerity and authenticity. It is free of political themes, unsentimental, and truthful.

Key 61   E. E. Cummings (1894–1962)

OVERVIEW   *E. E. Cummings was one of the Modernist poets who began to publish in the 1920s. Unlike his older contemporaries—Pound, Eliot, and Stevens—what he wrote about was not new, but the manner of his expression was unprecedented, giving familiar ideas freshness and the emotional impact of surprise. His success in making poetry a verbal game kept this spokesman for the sentiments of an earlier era in the public eye well into the 1950s.*

Themes: His poems celebrate spontaneity and an uncritical enthusiasm for life.
- As a pure romantic, he distrusted knowledge rationally acquired and relied only on his emotions and the intuitions they disclosed.
- Consequently his poems celebrate the beauty of nature, of love, sex, and lovers and the vivid life they enjoy. Children, country people, and even city eccentrics, their ability to feel not blunted by cynicism, are also among the good of the earth.
- On the other hand his poems hold up to contempt war and warmakers, the scheming rich, the complacent bourgeoisie, the ignorant and unimaginative "mostpeople," and those who depend on rationality and the intellect: scientists, philosophers, political theorists, especially labor leaders, New Dealers, and Communists.

Poetic method: The poems intentionally distort the language to force the reader to solve its puzzles and, succeeding, to experience the shock of recognition.
- There are few difficult ideas, but imagination is required to fill in ellipses in such a line as "What if a much of a which if a wind..." and (in the same poem) resolve the paradoxes of "Blow soon to never and never to twice."
- Cummings turns verbs into nouns, adverbs into adjectives, scrambles spelling as in "r-p-o-p-h-e-s-s-a-g-r" (a grasshopper gathering itself for a leap).
- He breaks words to be rejoined later, and uses punctuation and unconventional typography to enhance an image or control the rhythm and speed of lines.
- The same tricks recur, and with a little practice they are easily mastered.

Poems:

- The early poem "Thy Fingers Make Early Flowers" shows Cummings using turn-of-the-century versification and pre-Raphaelite imagery to state prettily the idea that love transforms all it touches to beauty and validates life, however short.

- "In Just-," from the same period, treats the theme of love again, but the verbal tricks are beginning to emerge as Cummings celebrates the moment in the spring of the year and the spring of life when children turn from play to answer the call of the Dionysian "goat-footed / balloonMan" who "whistles / far / and / wee," punning with "wee" on the French word "oui" to suggest sexual consent.

- In "Buffalo Bill's Defunct" the death of a popular hero is turned into an imagist poem, ending with imagism's characteristic misty hint of some elusive significance.

- In "My Sweet Old Etcetera," a soldier in the trenches of World War I muses with mild mockery on his family's enthusiastic response to the war, playing on multiple implications of "etcetera," coming at last to what is really on his mind—his girlfriend's "…smile / eyes knees and…Etcetera."

- Cummings' hatred of war gives us for a hero "Olaf glad and big," a conscientious objector, passive under cruel hazing, who quietly declares, "I will not kiss your fucking flag," and "there is some shit. I will not eat," and without recanting dies in prison.

- "If There Are Any Heavens" shows Cummings' love for his mother with nineteenth century sentimentality, but "My Father Moved Through Dooms of Love" is redeemed from the charge of sentimentality by being a better poem. Although Cummings' beloved earthly father is present here, he is apotheosized into something like God the Father and God the Son.

- Cummings' bias against organized labor and the welfare state is given with a grim cleverness in "When Serpents Bargain for the Right to Squirm."

Key 62   John Dos Passos (1896–1970)

OVERVIEW   *The best novels of John Dos Passos offer wide-screen views of great national and international events. Diminished against that vast background, his characters act out the events of their commonplace lives. The author's position is deeply informed, detached, and ironic. He writes, in effect, the social and moral history of the periods his novels cover.*

Themes: Dos Passos' themes remained the same throughout his life, but his attitude toward them shifted from the radical left to the conservative right: war, labor, politics, social justice, the masses, urban and industrialized society, the bases of our national power. The index against which he measured our society at any point in its history was the degree of personal freedom enjoyed by its citizens.

Method: Especially in his earlier work, the method is experimental. Since his screen is so wide, he contrived a variety of devices to fill it: in the straightforward language of literary naturalism he introduced popular songs, newspaper headlines, the public utterances of actual persons—political, industrial, financial, military—biographical vignettes of figures in the national eye, and so on. In his best known book, *U.S.A.*, in addition to these devices, recurrent segments called "The Camera Eye" comprise a sort of diary of Dos Passos himself at intervals in his life.

U.S.A.: A trilogy—*The Forty-Second Parallel* (1930), *1919* (1932), *The Big Money* (1936). As the title suggests, the protagonist of the trilogy is America itself. Beginning just before World War I, *U.S.A.* sweeps through major national events to the middle of the Great Depression. The characters whose lives are the subject of the "novels" within the larger work disappoint the hope for a redeeming social revolution by their triviality and weakness. *The Big Money* ends on a despairing note for America's future.

Key 63   F. Scott Fitzgerald (1896–1940)

OVERVIEW   *F. Scott Fitzgerald called the 1920s "The Jazz Age." His fiction told the story of this period and thereby defined it, while at the same time he and his talented but unstable wife Zelda led lives like those of his wealthy and glamorous characters. To support his extravagance Fitzgerald wrote a great quantity of magazine fiction, most of which will not survive. The fine remainder which he consciously differentiated from his potboilers will endure.*

Stories and novels:

The Great Gatsby (1925): Jay Gatsby believes passionately that by piling up great wealth and its material symbols and setting on top of the pile the young woman he had loved and lost a few years earlier he can redeem the past and give it the happiest of endings.
- With Daisy at last seated beside him, the material finishing touch to his magnificent house, the magic in which he had been confident fails and Gatsby's Great American Dream collapses.
- His murder seals this fatal blow to his spirit.

Tender Is the Night (1934): This novel criticizes both the connection between wealth and happiness and our infatuation with youth.
- Dick Diver, a brilliant American psychiatrist at a Swiss sanitorium, marries his immensely wealthy young American patient, Nicole Warren.
- Her money leads him within a few years to abandon his profession and in a Riviera villa indulge his refined tastes.
- There a teenage Hollywood star, Rosemary Hoyt, falls in love with this 35-year-old master of living, a father-figure to her as he had been to the incestuously abused Nicole.
- He responds to her youth as he had to Nicole's and is torn between his love for both.
- But Rosemary outgrows her crush and Nicole in becoming well outgrows her dependency.
- Dick, alone and no longer moored to his profession, drifts into obscurity.

"Winter Dreams": This early story, not representative of the best of Fitzgerald's short fiction, foreshadows both of the great novels.
- Dexter Green makes money enough to win the golden girl, Judy

Jones, but pursuing Jazz Age excitements she evades commitment.
- She and he marry—but not each other and unwisely.
- When subsequent events seem to offer Dexter, as they did Gatsby, a chance to retrieve the past, time and the smudging of life itself have blurred the glory of Judy Jones as they did Rosemary Hoyt and Dexter for all his money is left, like Dick Diver, with nothing.

"The Rich Boy": Anson Hunter is protected by his money from the need to make a commitment in love when the moment for commitment arrives. Consequently, through the ethical carelessness his wealth encourages, he loses Paula, the love of his life, and thereafter drifts emotionally through ever less genuine attachments into a limbo of the heart.

"Babylon Revisited": A more subdued story appropriate to its setting in Depression-muted Paris, it shows Charley Wales recovering from the dissipation of both his financial and moral capital in the debauched 1920s.
- Charley's immediate problem is to persuade the sister of his dead wife to give him custody of the 9-year-old daughter he fiercely loves.
- The sister is nearly persuaded of the truth—that Charley is at last a responsible person—when two drunken friends out of his alcoholic past appear like the Eumenides of Greek drama.
- The sister draws back sharply, and Charley leaves with penance more to do before he has his heart's desire.

Key 64   William Faulkner (1897–1962)

OVERVIEW   *Born to a distinguished Mississippi family, Faulkner had his first critical success in 1929 with the novel* The Sound and the Fury. *His 15 novels that tell the imagined saga of a "Yoknapatawpha County" in northwest Mississippi from the 1820s to the 1950s were not conceived as a fictionalized history of the region. They do, nevertheless, create in their totality, a powerful myth of the rise of the planter society, its defeat in the Civil War, and the consequences of that defeat among all classes.*

Narrative method: With some exceptions, the novels are written in a dense-textured, often experimental style, that makes demands on the reader's intelligence, memory, and reading skill. Faulkner often tells his stories in "stream of consciousness."

Themes:
- "The truths of the heart": strong feeling is a more reliable moral guide than the intellect.
- The sanctity of "the central 'I-am' ": the core of the personality, the irreducible basis for self-esteem, must never be violated by another person.
- The myth of a glamorous Southern past is an illusion.
- Racial prejudice is founded not on actual experience of whites with blacks but on an abstract idea of "negritude."
- The iniquity of the institution of slavery from the beginning condemned the South to eventual catastrophe.
- Living in harmony with wild nature can create in the individual religious vision and virtue.
- Virtue is not the monopoly of any race or class.
- Acquisitiveness ungoverned by a moral tradition dehumanizes.
- In "Wash," (1934) closely related to the novel *Absalom, Absalom!* (1936), the planter Thomas Sutpen is killed for his arrogant disregard for the feelings of Wash Jones, a poor white and of his daughter Millie.
- "That Evening Sun" (1931) shows the Compson family at an early moment in the moral decline that culminates in *The Sound and the Fury* (1931).

- "Barn Burning" (1931) establishes Ab Snopes' reputation as an arsonist, upon which his son Flem, in *The Hamlet*, (1940) capitalizes; and "Spotted Horses" (1931) gives a very funny example of Flem's tactics in exploiting his fellow man.
- "The Bear," a section from *Go Down Moses* (1942), principally concerns young Isaac McCaslin, heir to the McCaslin plantation, who acquires through years of wilderness hunting the virtues of courage, honor, pride, pity, and love of freedom and justice.

Key 65   Ernest Hemingway (1899–1961)

OVERVIEW   *Ernest Hemingway wrote ten novels and nearly seventy short storeis. The most important of the novels are* The Sun Also Rises *(1926),* A Fairewell to Arms *(1929) and* For Whom the Bell Tolls *(1940). With this body of work he created an admired and widely imitated prose style with which he depicted the modern world as stripped of illusion, psychologically and physically dangerous, and living beneath the shadow of moral ruin.*

Narrative method: The early work, done in the 1920s, is notable for the simplicity of its diction and sentence structure, in which coordinate clauses keep the narrative parts free from the value judgments implied by subordination.
- In the 1930s the sentence structure grew more complex, while retaining the unpretentious diction and the remarkable clarity of the earlier work.
- Hemingway continued to convey his characters' feelings by showing "the sequence of fact and motion that made the emotion" rather than by mere assertion.
- Generally achieving his effects by irony rather than symbolism, most of what he expresses in his fiction lies beneath the surface of the page.

Themes: Concerned with action and feeling rather than with reflective thought, Hemingway writes of love and its loss, of death and its avoidance.
- Consequently, passion and sex, war and crime, and the violence of blood sports predominate as his subject matter.
- Ideal conduct discloses grace under physical and psychological pressure, while the hero, aware of what he is up against ("the conditions of heroism"), acts in conformity to an ethical code.

Stories:
- The young and solitary trout fisherman of "Big Two-Hearted River" is wary of too much emotion as he hooks and lands big trout. An unspecified threat hangs over him, kept at bay by the sport and by his snug tent. But beneath the vivid surface of the story lies the trauma of battle shock waiting to repossess him.
- The terrors and satisfactions of hunting dangerous animals and the destructive power of marital disloyalty are the themes of "The

Short Happy Life of Francis Macomber." Macomber, disgraced by his public cowardice in a lion hunt and unmanned by his wife's contempt, learns from the safari guide that "we owe God a death." He redeems himself in action, but his "short happy life" of about fifteen minutes ends when his wife, ostensibly in an effort to save him from an infuriated cape buffalo, sends a bullet through his brain.

- In "The Snows of Kilimanjaro" Harry Streeter, a writer dying in East Africa of gangrene, recapitulates in his mind a life filled with action, a source of yet-unwritten fiction. Married for some years to a wealthy woman, he has neglected his work in a life of ease and self-indulgence, a gangrene of the spirit. Now it is too late. Death, the hyena, "wedge-headed and stinking," is almost at the side of his safari cot. In his delirium a rescue plane seems to carry him toward the snow-capped peak of Kilimanjaro where the frozen carcass of a leopard lies, symbol of the austere aspiration that had once made Harry an artist, a dedication he returns to only at the moment of death.

Key 66　Hart Crane (1899–1932)

OVERVIEW　*Hart Crane's poems, often obscure, found a limited audience. He was a perfectionist and a "poet's poet." Accursed by a wretched childhood, he died a suicide at 32, leaving behind remarkable short lyrics, a few longer poems, and a major American epic,* The Bridge *(1930). Although he lived in the pessimistic current of high Modernism, his epic is in the optimistic tradition of Emerson and Whitman, a conscious reply to Eliot and "The Waste Land."*

Themes: Unity in diversity; the sea; the modern city; American history as myth; ecstasy as the implied object of living; death and transcendence; the universality of the divine spirit.

Method: He frequently abandoned the logic of language in an attempt to produce in the reader a felt rather than an understood response.
- One result of this aim was language of an extraordinary density and poems often impossible to paraphrase.
- He depended on the image to create the Modernist "intellectual and emotional complex in a moment of time."
- He charged his poems (especially *The Bridge*) with symbols that change into other shapes while retaining their original significance.
- He wrote in a wide variety of forms, from blank verse to jazz rhythms.

Poems:
- "At Melville's Tomb" alludes to *Moby Dick* and Ahab's vision of the sea floor, littered with victims of nature in its malicious aspect, an "embassy" that led Melville to ultimate profundities of metaphysical thought and reconciliation with the cosmos.
- "Voyages" reflect in their gorgeous imagery Crane's delight in the Caribbean, where his sailor-lover ("my Prodigal") roamed, and his anguished spirit experienced intervals of ecstasy.
- *The Bridge*, a long epic in eight sections, extends the arc of a circle that is the Brooklyn Bridge westward across America until it comes to symbolize unity—human and divine. A succession of vignettes include Rip Van Winkle, Christopher Columbus, hoboes riding the rods, the Mississippi and the life along its banks, Pocahontas and the lore of Native Americans, pioneer settlers, the great clipper ships, and so on. The stories create a partial history, a Romantic myth that affirms a faith in the American future.

Key 67 Thomas Wolfe (1900–1938)

OVERVIEW *In four long novels and nearly 60 short stories Thomas Wolfe combines autobiography and invention to create literary art. No matter whether he calls his hero Eugene Gant or Monk Webber he is the persona of Thomas Wolfe. The short stories are almost entirely narratives cut from the novels.*

Narrative method: After his first novel, *Look Homeward, Angel* (1929), Wolfe planned to pattern his novels on classical myth, but when he began writing, he fell back on the chronology of autobiography. Writing in a prose that is poetically rhythmic and luxuriant in diction, he achieves powerful effects, but the achievement is often marred by verbosity and excessive rhetoric.

Themes: Wolfe's heroes are engaged in the romantic quest for self knowledge, and in that quest they attempt to satisfy an insatiable appetite for experience.
- The outward explorations of the questing hero create a counter movement homeward as he seeks rest from wandering, his father, and the beauty of the American earth.
- **Time**, where all memory exists, can be retrieved only by its recreation in the mind and imagination of the artist.

Stories:
- "An Angel on the Porch" (Wolfe's first published story, excerpted from *Look Homeward, Angel*) sets against the pulsing life of a North Carolina mountain city the purchased marble angel, symbol of the never-fulfilled aspiration of the stonecutter, Oliver Gant, to create with his own chisel; of desire (now all but dead), and of death and all loss that comes with the passage of time.
- "The Lost Boy," perhaps Wolfe's finest story, begins in the same town square, moves through Gant's marble shop, as the narrator, Gant's son Eugene (the same consciousness that told the story of the angel), seeks in memory a cherished older brother, dead in childhood, to retrieve the past and a part of the self. Where Gant has failed, his son has achieved the power to create. The story we read is the evidence.

Key 68   Langston Hughes (1902–1976)

OVERVIEW   *Hughes was the leading writer of the Harlem Renaissance of the 1920s. His strong influence on young black writers was mainly as a poet, but he wrote successfully in all literary forms. He urged black writers to be true to their roots, to aim at pleasing neither black nor white readers but to use with absolute honesty the material of their black experience. His work, with its authentic folk elements, set an excellent example.*

Themes: Black aspiration repressed is explosive; jazz transforms black pain into beauty; the new African-American generation must continue the upward struggle; black people have been a part of many cultures, from the most ancient to the modern; exuberance, joy, and beauty exist in black life along with the anguish.

Method: In poetry a variety of forms: conventional stanzas and rhymes, free verse, a hybrid free verse with interspersed rhymes, prose-poetry. Frequent use of dialect. Frequent use of jazz rhythms—blues, bebop, rap. In fiction: most notably the use of the black "folk-speaker" in dialogue with an anonymous respondent.

Poems:
- "The Negro Speaks of Rivers" asserts the richness of black culture.
- "Mother to Son" admonishes black youth to climb, not rest.
- "Motto" offers a practical formula for survival in the black world: savor life, but keep a low profile.
- "Trumpet Player" transmutes the sting of racial memory and the pain of deprivation to gold.
- "Harlem" says "the dream deferred" may explode in violence.
- The lynched young lover of "Song for a Dark Girl" is crucified in a world where God seems absent.

Prose sketches: In five books, beginning in 1950 with *Simple Speaks His Mind,* Hughes created a series of sketches offering the folk wit and wisdom of Jesse B. Simple, a black man of the modern city. With genial but effective satire, "Simple" exposes white dishonesty and injustice while exposing some amusing shortcomings of his own.

Essay: In "The Artist and the Racial Mountain" Hughes makes a passionate plea to young black artists to draw upon their own black experience, undiluted by white elements.

Key 69   John Steinbeck (1902–1968)

OVERVIEW   *John Steinbeck had his greatest success during the Depression of the 1930s. Although in the 1940s the quality of his work declined, he was awarded the Nobel Prize for Literature in 1962 for his overall distinction.*

Subject matter: His fiction tells with compassion the stories of Americans pushed by economic forces to the margins of society—the drifters, the outcasts, the migratory workers, the primitives. His work prescribed no social program but expresses a faith in the common people to use political democracy in a radical way to improve their condition as a class.

Themes: Steinbeck was a literary naturalist whose poor and unschooled men and women contend with forces too strong for them—forces rooted in prejudice, custom, tradition, and long-established social attitudes, in privilege and injustice, in a market-driven economy, and in genetics, hunger, and the sex drive. The three novels for which Steinbeck is best known treat all of these themes: *In Dubious Battle* (1936), *Of Mice and Men* (1937), and his masterpiece, *The Grapes of Wrath* (1939).

Stories:
- "Flight" tells of Pepe Torres, 19, perhaps defective genetically, perhaps simply retarded by ignorance and poverty on a farm isolated on the southern California coast. He is not, therefore, wholly accountable for his acts. And similarly, when his honor is threatened, not his will but his Hispanic temperament reacts with murderous violence, and Pepe must take flight. In the mountains, indifferent nature makes it easy for vengeance to be exacted by his invisible pursuers carrying out without reflection the imperatives of their ancient culture.
- "The Leader of the People" tells of an old man who in his younger days heroically led a wagon train west to the Pacific. Only his grandson now willingly listens to his tale of the one achievement of a long life whose thrust was literally arrested by the ocean. Steinbeck equates the westering impulse with a national aspiration toward some indistinctly felt ideal now lost in our commonplace existence.

Key 70 Richard Wright (1908–1960)

OVERVIEW *Richard Wright was the first African-American writer to win a broad response from the reading public. Struggling against his Southern birth and deprived upbringing with talent, character, and courage, his growing awareness of the oppressed condition of his race made him a Communist and a journalist for the Communist cause. Determined to write fiction, he published a book of stories, followed by a novel,* Native Son *(1940). With its publication he became a leading American novelist. When in 1944 he realized that he and his people were being cynically manipulated by the Party for its own larger purposes, he ended his affiliation.*

Themes: Racism, latent black rage, determinism in underclass black life, white hypocrisy and dishonesty, radical politics.

Method: Realistic literary naturalism. The narrative advances chronologically through a series of dramatic episodes. Ideas are expressed by what characters do or say or through symbols that emerge naturally from the narrative.

Native Son (1940): Bigger Thomas, a black youth from a Chicago ghetto, is given a job as a chauffeur in the home of a liberal white philanthropist. One late night, with ambiguous intentions, Bigger carries the drunken and unconscious daughter of his employer from her car to her bedroom. To avoid discovery by the girl's blind mother, Bigger stifles the girl's drunken mumbling and unintentionally smothers her. Ferociously pursued by the police, he is caught, tried, convicted, and executed. During Bigger's trial, Max, his radical defender, shows how the forces surrounding Bigger's birth and short life made his crime and death inevitable.

Stories:
- In "The Man Who Was Almost a Man" (1939), a black farm boy acquires a pistol to give himself manly confidence. Subconsciously he is raging with unfocused hatred. Fleeing the consequences of his innocent misadventures with the pistol, he hops a freight thinking ominously that he is heading "away to somewhere, somewhere where he could be a man…"

- In "Big Black Good Man" a frightened night clerk of a Copenhagen waterfront hotel procures whiskey and a whore for a giant black sailor for each night of a week's stay. When the giant checks out he circles the clerk's neck with his hands and the clerk's week-long fear becomes pure terror. No harm results, however. The clerk's misperception is corrected when the grateful giant returns a year later with six shirts for the clerk, all with the correct collar size.

Theme 7 CULTURAL DIVERSITY IN AMERICAN LITERATURE, 1945–1980

*I*n the early 1940s criticism placed a new emphasis on the purely literary aspects of writing and insisted that the artist worked outside of political and social considerations. This position became controversial in the 1960s and, from the 1970s to the present, has been the object of increasingly vigorous attack. Beginning with the women's liberation movement of the 1970s, literature came under the scrutiny of feminist, gay, African-American, Native-American, and Marxist criticism. The political content of such writers as Adrienne Rich, Alan Ginsberg, James Baldwin, and Alice Walker was counted among their virtues. Seen in the long view, however, most writers continued to write within the tradition of Emerson and Whitman, recurring to the great American myths of upward mobility, the melting pot, and a free and enlightened nation.

INDIVIDUAL KEYS IN THIS THEME

Key 71   Eudora Welty (1909–   )

OVERVIEW   *Eudora Welty is a Southern regional realist. Her pictures of twentieth-century life in rural and small town Mississippi accurately reflect both its surfaces and its deeper psychological currents. She is fond of her characters, and their petty malice is always comically rendered. But despite her affection for humankind, she has always stood well outside of politics and causes.*

Themes: Manners and folkways in the middle-class South, the attachment to older ways, and the resistance to change by individuals and communities.

Method: Occasionally experimental in the use of myth and archetypal situations, her work reflects the oral tradition of Southern storytelling.

Stories:
- "Why I Live at the P.O." (1940) is told in the first person by the young postmistress "of the next to smallest P.O. in the entire state of Mississippi." Eccentricity reigns in a family where envy, jealousy, and resentment provoke comic quarrels and drive the more than mildly paranoid narrator out of the house to "live at the P.O."
- "The Petrified Man" (1941) tells of malicious gossip, trivial greed, and conscienceless inhumanity, amidst the vulgarity of a small town beauty salon. Although all the characters and their situations are unpleasant, the ironies of the story, its regionalisms, and the amused tolerance of the author make it funny.

Key 72   Ralph Ellison (1914–   )

OVERVIEW   *Ellison resists being categorized as a black writer, aiming in his fiction to address the universal human condition. His only novel to date,* Invisible Man, *is a satirical treatment of the black experience but, says his unnamed protagonist, "Who knows but that, on the lower frequencies, I may speak for you." The novel won the National Book Award when it was published in 1952 and is regarded as a classic of modern American literature.*

Themes: Black-white relationships; African-American social, ethnic, regional, and moral traditions treated critically and satirically; the cynicism with which the white establishment on the one hand and the Communist Party on the other manipulate African-Americans—with black complicity.

Method: Realism, with its limitations greatly extended through symbolism and the interweaving of expressionistic and surrealistic scenes and situations. Rich-textured rhetoric, a style charged with energy and exuberance.

***Invisible Man*:** Born in the deep South, the unnamed first-person narrator of the novel early adopts the compliant behavior of what the whites around him call a "good Negro," his individualism "invisible."

- Educated at a small black college whose president is in league with its white benefactors, he is sent north to powerful whites who intend to place him in positions with titles that are high-sounding but empty of substance, to keep him "invisible." He discovers the imposture and pitches himself into what for him is the chaos of New York City.

- After a bewildering succession of adventures in which he is manipulated by communists, labor-haters, a psychiatrist, a sex-obsessed white woman, and a mad black nationalist, he flees into the world of Harlem hipsters.

- Running for his life he falls into a coal cellar. Perceiving at last the world's absurdity he determines to remain underground and to write down the events (the novel itself) that have carried him to this illumination.

Chapter I of the novel *(Battle Royal)*: The narrator, his high school's valedictorian, is invited to address a businessmen's group at a smoker in a downtown hotel.

- He arrives and is coerced into a blindfolded boxing match with nine of his black classmates but only after they are forced to watch a blond erotic dancer, an American flag tattooed on her belly, perform.
- When he is called upon to speak his mouth is bloody from the battle royal."Social responsibility" comes out "social equality," creating a furor among his listeners who are only reluctantly persuaded his language was inadvertent.
- At last given his reward, a calfskin briefcase with a college scholarship certificate inside, he dreams that night of finding also inside an engraved document that reads, "To Whom It May Concern: Keep This Nigger-Boy Running."

Key 73 Saul Bellow (1915–)

OVERVIEW *Perhaps foremost among the American novelists who came into prominence after World War II, 1976 Nobel Laureate Bellow is part of the novelistic mainstream, bringing to that tradition fresh imagination, wisdom in human affairs, and an impressive erudition. His books have the rich flavor of his urban Jewish upbringing. Although considered an American writer Bellow was actually born in Quebec Province in Canada, spending his early childhood in the poor district of Montreal. He moved with his family to Chicago in 1924.*

Themes: Bellow's characters are frequently in search of their own identity.
- They are rootless, or more often find themselves in situations where their roots are irrelevant.
- Pressed on all sides by the city's masses they struggle to assert their individuality and humanity.
- Even when defeated they hold tenaciously to some remnant of human dignity.

Novels:
- Bellow emerged as a major writer in 1953 with *The Adventures of Augie March*, a picaresque "novel of development" that follows Augie from his boyhood and youth in Chicago, through Mexico, to manhood in Paris, his quest for identity still unresolved.
- The humor that from this time forward complements the pathos of Bellow's situations touches his 1956 Freudian novella *Seize the Day*, where Tommy Wilhelm, sympathetic and admirable though fated to fail, courts success to get the attention of the unloving father he adores. Despair, self-loathing, guilt, grief for lost love, plunge him into mourning over the corpse of a man he has never before seen, a surrogate both for himself and his father.
- In *Henderson the Rain King* (1959) an American millionaire goes to Africa in a mythic search for spiritual power, becomes a rainmaker and heir to a throne.
- *Herzog* (1964) is a dazzling display of Bellow's erudition as he discloses the intellectual inner life of the love-stricken Moses Herzog.

- *Mr. Sammler's Planet* (1970) gives us the thoughts of a Holocaust survivor on the Earth's future in what is sometimes called Bellow's best novel.
- *Humboldt's Gift* (1975), through the desperate story of a professor-writer, Charlie Citrine, discloses the tragic life of Von Humboldt Fleischer, a character closely modeled on the American poet, Delmore Schwartz.

Stories:

- In "Looking for Mr. Green," George Grebe, a college graduate with a stop-gap Depression job, delivers relief checks to handicapped blacks. Reminded by his supervisor of the theological-philosophical concept that this is a "fallen world of appearances," he finds in the phantasmagoria of slip-sliding reality in the black slums the truth that this world is indeed fallen, but that "appearances" of poverty and degradation are real enough.
- In "A Silver Dish," the middle-aged Morris Selbst, chiseler, petty gambler, adulterer, conscienceless exploiter of his family, steals a silver dish from a philanthropic woman to make her pay for the kindness she is about to bestow upon him: $50. "Kind has a price tag," he tells his son, Woody, and with the theft Morris preserves some shred of whatever dignity remains to him.

Key 74   Tennessee Williams (1911–1983)

OVERVIEW   *From the end of World War II to his accidental death in 1983 Williams shared with Arthur Miller the distinction of foremost American dramatist. Beginning with* The Glass Menagerie *in 1945, he wrote more than two plays a year for 15 years, almost all of which were both commercial and critical successes. He often revised existing plays, produced or unproduced, to create new plays. His plays are notable for their fusion of the realistic and the non-realistic.*

Themes: As time passes, losses always accrue; the struggle to preserve personal values; the outsider or fugitive in a hostile group; the ambiguity of morality; the search for relief from the anguish of life; fear of dying and a longing to live.

Method: Psychological realism and realism of setting combined with anti-realistic devices:
- Dialogue mixed with direct address, soliloquy, and confession.
- Isolation of characters during set speeches by lighting.
- Projection of words and pictures to explain or elaborate the action.
- Frequent use of symbols and significant names and of music to enhance mood.

Plays:
- Amanda, in *The Glass Menagerie* (1945), is a Southern lady living in poverty among delusions of a gentle past. She imposes her claim to gentility upon her children, Tom and Laura, driving Tom off to sea and with the best of intentions creating a situation that emotionally crushes Laura, fragile as her glass animals.
- *A Streetcar Named Desire* (1947) is another dramatization of Southern decay. Blanche DuBois comes for an extended visit to her sister Stella, happily married to the boorish and violent Stanley Kowalski and living in a shabby corner of New Orleans. An alcoholic nymphomaniac with a lurid past, an aristocrat in sharp decline, Blanche disturbs the equilibrium of Stanley and Stella and their poker-playing, beer-drinking friends. Deeply neurotic on her arrival and persecuted by a hostile Stanley as a threat to his marriage, Blanche declines into psychosis and, in the final scene, is taken away in a straitjacket.

Key 75　Arthur Miller (1915–　)

OVERVIEW　*Miller shares with Tennessee Williams the distinction of being the best American dramatist of the period from the end of World War II to the present. While their quality is equivalent, Williams' plays are based on emotion, Miller's on ethical ideas.*

Themes: The ethical struggle between right and wrong; the need for mankind to struggle against deterministic forces; the American myth of success; the dehumanization of modern society; individual responsibility; the generation gap; brothers with contrasting values; the individual conforming to or resisting social values; significance disclosed through the death of a character following breakdown.

Method: Ibsenesque realism (*All My Sons*); romantic or lyrical realism (*A View From the Bridge*); expressionism (*Death of a Salesman*); allegory (*The Crucible*).

Plays:
- In *All My Sons* (1947) the business practices of manufacturer Joe Keller conflict with the ethics of his fiercely loved son, Chris, a conflict that ends with Joe's suicide.
- *Death of a Salesman* (1949) is the tragedy of Willy Loman who dies from the dehumanizing effect of his unwavering pursuit of business success and his never-extinguished faith in the power of appearance and personality.
- In *A View From the Bridge* (1955) Eddie Carbone violates the code of ethnic loyalty in his Brooklyn neighborhood and provokes his own death when he is unable to accept the label of informer.
- Seventeenth century Salem labels John Proctor a witch in *The Crucible* (1953). Refusing to make a false confession or to save himself by implicating others, Proctor dies a hero in a play seen as an allegory of the McCarthy witch-hunt of the 1950s.
- The characters in *A Memory of Two Mondays* (1955) speak in a variety of dialects as they perform their dehumanizing tasks in an auto-parts warehouse and thus can be seen as representative of humanity at large.

Key 76   James Baldwin (1924–1987)

OVERVIEW   *James Baldwin's first novel,* Go Tell It on the Mountain *(1953) placed him along with Ralph Ellison in the forefront of African-American writers of the day. The next five novels were less successful. His principal distinction was as a spokesman for his people. His journalism of the 1950s and '60s was directed with great effectiveness at the conscience of America.* The Fire Next Time *(1963) provoked an even more ardent response from white readers than from black and is judged to have had a powerful impact on the civil rights legislation that followed.*

Themes: Social injustice, the black experience in America, the struggle of African-Americans for self-realization, anti-separatism as a political principle, Christian love as the means whereby African-Americans can begin healing the rift between black and white America.

Method: Baldwin was not a literary experimenter like Ellison. Naturalistic realism served all of his fictional needs.

Go Tell It on the Mountain: Relates the struggle of an intelligent and sensitive boy to transcend his Harlem environment and the religious fundamentalism of his family to arrive at the edge of self-realization.

"Sonny's Blues" (1956): A young Harlem schoolteacher comes to understand his ex-junkie, ex-con brother when, in a Greenwich Village night spot at the piano with a jazz quartet, Sonny plays the pain, despair, rage, love, and vision of beauty that explain him and thousands like him.

Journalism: With eloquence and power *The Fire Next Time* sets forth the injustices, indignities, humiliations, and agonies that are the common experience of African-Americans. These hideous disfigurations of American society can be repaired only by the Christian love of the victims themselves for their white brothers. This painful act and the renunciation of the temptation to withdraw into black separatism are possible partly because African-Americans do not accept the myths of American history that sustain white America's self-image.

Key 77 Flannery O'Connor (1925–1964)

OVERVIEW *Flannery O'Connor was a devout Catholic from the rural Protestant South. Her Catholicism rarely emerges explicitly, but her intense piety arranges and resolves the situations she contrives for characters who are frequently grotesque, often eccentric, even dull and decent, sinisterly secularlized, or genuinely satanic. Her fiction is charged with a violence both comical and terrifying. She places her characters in the hands of a God whose justice seems appalling by worldly standards but sublime under the aspect of eternity.*

Narrative method: Only occasionally resorting to dialect, O'Connor, like Faulkner before her and Mark Twain before him, conveys the sound of rural Southern speech by the words her characters use and the order in which they use them.
- Her ear for the cliches that express what passes for their thought lets her sketch the moral landscape of her region in a way that is both funny and convincing.
- Her fiction is allegorical and parabolic, and her symbolic use of bread, water, and fire discloses to us a vision of violent apocalypse.

"The Life You Save May Be Your Own" (1955) is the story of the Craters, mother and daughter, and Tom Shiftlet. The title reflects the highway signs hanging "Drive carefully the life you save may be your own." Such self-interest motivates Shiftlet.
- In a travesty on biblical miracles he teaches the mute daughter to speak and raises from the dead the mother's old car.
- To acquire the car he marries the retarded girl, abandons her at a roadside joint, and drives away, suffering a fantasy of guilt in which as an inverted Christ he confuses his blonde and blue-eyed bride with his mother abandoned long ago. His hallucination turns the girl into the Virgin Mary, now sleeping with her head on the counter of "The Hot Spot," vulnerable and unprotected.
- In a hell of deluded self-righteousness he calls on God to wash away the slime of the earth and God, with a Jovian chuckle-rumble, obliges and Shiftlet is washed on the edge of a deluge into Mobile.

"A Good Man Is Hard to Find": A family vacation begins in contention and petty cruelty and ends in horror.
- As they drive along the highway, the young parents and their small

children, are so fixed in the most banal elements of popular culture that they cannot enjoy the landscape.

- The decent grandmother, trying her best to amuse the spoiled children, calls their attention to a "pickaninny" standing before a paintless cabin, naked but for his undershirt. The child is a part of a landscape she has always known and accepted without reflection. The children stare in contempt and return to their quarrel.
- Later, with their car overturned beside the embankment of a lonely road, they come under the power of three sociopaths on a killing spree. One by one the family is taken into the woods and shot.
- To the still-surviving grandmother the leader of the murderous three explains that had he seen Christ living, he could have believed, but failing that, "there ain't no pleasure but in meanness."
- With a pistol against her heart, her family dead, the old woman's mind swims. "Why, I know you!" she says, "You're one of my babies," and as she reaches to touch with love the cheek of "the Misfit" he pulls the trigger.
- At the hour of her death she has without intending it found the "good man," Christ, and in the finding discovered her love for all created being that in the mystical moment includes, of course, the little pickaninny.

"Good Country People": Satan appears in the form of an unctuous young bible salesman who comes to the well-to-do farm of the divorced Mrs. Hopewell and her crippled Ph.D. daughter, Hulga.

- Mrs. Hopewell's ethics rest on sentimental tolerance and bland good will. Her daughter's ethics are based on a sophisticated and materialistic rationalism.
- Both the easygoing mother and the intellectually arrogant daughter are deceived by the bible salesman, whose evil cannot be detected by either moral outlook.
- With Hulga's "soul" (her "wooden leg") in his suitcase and while Mrs. Hopewell unconcernedly cultivates a patch of onions (traditionally potent against baleful spirits) the bible salesman disappears "under the hill" abandoning Hulga, helpless and outrageously humiliated in a remote hayloft.
- The complacent mother will find the notion of "good country people" to be a foolish myth.

Wise Blood (1952): The first of O'Connor's two novels uses the theme of "the hound of heaven" to tell the story of Haze Motes (whose name suggests impaired spiritual vision) and his unsuccessful attempt to deny his heritage: to refuse to play Elisha to the Elijah of his circuit-preacher grandfather; to evade the "wild ragged figure" of Jesus and found "the Church Without Christ."

- Despite his furious denial of Christian belief, his "glare blue" suit softens to the blue of Mary's mantle and his garish white Panama takes on the light brown of sacramental wheat.
- An angel in the guise of a highway patrolman pushes Motes' "high, rat-colored car" into a deep gully, thus destroying the temple of the Church Without Christ.
- Succumbing to the irresistible grace of God, Haze blinds himself as an act of faith, walks with stones in his shoes, and sleeps with barbed wire binding his chest.
- He exists in darkness and dies with only a pinpoint of light before him, but that pinpoint is the star of Bethlehem.

The Violent Bear It Away (1960): Her second novel returns to the theme of "the hound of heaven" but gives the theme a more fully developed treatment and adds the theme implied in "Good Country People": the conflict between rational knowledge and the insight immediately imparted to the soul by the spirit of God.
- Like Haze Motes, Tarwater inherits from a relative the imperative to walk "in the bleeding stinking mad shadow of Jesus" and the "wise blood" of the prophet. And like Haze he fights impotently against God's grace.
- Leaving their backcountry farm at the death of the great-uncle who raised him to prophesy, he heads for the city. There he moves in with his uncle Rayber.
- Rayber fights his own wise blood by worshipping rational knowledge, and there Tarwater finds the idiot cousin he must against all reason baptize.
- For Flannery O'Connor the Christian sacraments were not merely symbolic but literal transactions between God and man, valid regardless of conscious intention.
- Tarwater drowns his little cousin in a country lake that seems divinely set there for the purpose, but, unwilling as Jonah, he fulfills God's command. Immersed in water he "accidentally" pronounces the words of baptism and as O'Connor would have it, saves an immortal soul.
- Returning to the farm, he is surprised to find that in the farmhouse fire he set, his great-uncle has not been cremated but given proper Christian burial by an angel of God, a local black farmer.
- Capitulating at last to God's irresistible grace, Elisha-Tarwater accepts the mantle of Elijah, his great-uncle, and turns again "toward the dark city, where the children of God lay sleeping."

Key 78   John Barth (1930–   )

OVERVIEW   *Barth is one of a number of post-Modernist writers (see Key 80, Thomas Pynchon) of "self-reflexive" fiction. Like them, he has rejected the Modernist concern for who we are and why we behave as we do, turning fiction into an "irreal" entertainment that examines the process whereby the fiction on the page before us is being created.*

Method: The "self-reflexive" writer is often a participant, a character in his own fiction, both acting within it and commenting upon it. The reader is frequently reminded directly or indirectly that what he is reading is a fabrication that has no significant connection with actual life.

Themes: The fragmentation of life; the loss of reasons for living; the utility of conscious role-playing in order to live *as if* motivated by genuine feeling; emotional paralysis; fiction as an entity existing by and for itself.

Novels:
- In *The Floating Opera* (1956) Todd Andrews spends ten years intensely analyzing the day he decided against suicide, concluding that there is no reason for choosing *either* life or death.
- *The End of the Road* (1958) places the emotionally paralyzed Horner under the care of a "doctor" who spins out stories of a number of lives Horner might choose to live and thus artificially resuscitate his own.
- Similarly, *The Sot-Weed Factor* (1967) uses the frontier freedom of colonial Maryland as a stage where any life can be chosen and thereafter lived as a work of art.

Stories:
- In "Lost in the Fun House" the narrator creates from memory and imagination a "real" fun house with "real" characters, including the narrator who imagines building his own fun house and (like a novelist) controlling from his electrical panel the effects, surprises, and illusions that determine the course of his characters through the fun house of life.
- "A Life" shows a writer who suspects himself of being a character in someone else's fiction writing a fiction in which a character he creates is also writing a fiction about yet another writer—and so on, perhaps, ad infinitum.

Key 79   John Updike (1932–   )

OVERVIEW   *John Updike is a "neo-realist" celebrated for the precision of his style and the painterly way he recreates the surfaces of his world. His fiction conveys his vision of middle America and of the middle class holding onto its style of life while at the same time trying to adjust its mind to new ideas and new social realities.*

Themes: Marriage and divorce, suburban and exurban life, married and adulterous sex, Christian faith, decline of the small town, adolescence and its striving toward autonomy.

Method: Traditional realistic naturalism conveyed with prose of great precision and clarity of expression in spite of its allusiveness and complexity. Genial satire, affection for his characters, an ironically humorous attitude toward their situations.

Novels:
- *Rabbit Run* (1960). Since his glory days of high school basketball, Rabbit Angstrom's life has gone gently downhill. He reacts to his growing despair by abandoning his mistress and his wife and child and running away into aimless drifting.
- *The Centaur* (1963) interweaves the story of a rural high school teacher and his student-son Peter with the myth of Chiron and his student Prometheus.
- *Couples* (1968) bares the intertwined sex-lives of an exurban group and in the interaction both sex and religion define each other.
- *Rabbit Redux* (1971) tries to give a coherent account of the political violence of the 1960s by filtering it through the consciousness of Rabbit Angstrom.

Stories:
- In "Pigeon Feathers" David's badly shaken religious faith is restored as the functional perfection and beauty of a dead pigeon's feathers assures him of the Creator's power and love.
- The young narrator of "The Happiest I've Been" finds unprecedented happiness in the trust implied when within a few hours a young woman falls asleep in his arms and a lifelong but equivocal friend not only for the first time lets him take the wheel of his car but falls asleep as they drive west on the freeway.

Key 80   Thomas Pynchon (1938–)

OVERVIEW   *A recluse last seen in 1963, Pynchon has written four satirical novels of brilliant, often hilarious, social criticism and a book of short stories. He sees our world as comically sinister, enmeshed in high technology, where men and women have been crippled, blighted, made grotesque, and dehumanized by science out of control.*

Themes: The failure of science to heal our spiritual sickness (for which it is responsible), the attempt of cybernetics to treat human beings as if they were machines, the quest for some dimly conceived good, the distorted values of our civilization, the inherent imprecision of language, the pain of our existence, the comedy of our predicament, freedom in contrast to life within contemporary institutions.

Method: Uses multiple plots involving ingeniously complicated events to mirror the chaos and anarchy of our lives; weaves the fantastic into his basic realism, mingling the ominous and threatening with the comedy inherent in our human weakness; treats his materials with wit and exuberance; plays the part of a universal hipster with apparently vast knowledge of the covert facts crucial to our very modern world.

Novels:
- *V* (1963) is a report on present-day existence, where to avoid anger and pain we disengage ourselves from life by modeling our behavior on the smoothly running communications devices that surround us. "V" (Venus, virgin, vagina, void?) is a woman who has become little more than an automatic response to erotic stimuli.
- *The Crying of Lot 49* (1966) is a kind of allegory in which the mysterious legacy that comes to sexy Mrs. Oedipa Maas comes to be seen as an American heritage so unwholesome that questing Oedipa turns up evidence of a turned-off segment of America, gone underground, communicating by a system they have contrived as a substitute for the U.S. Postal System.
- *Gravity's Rainbow* (1973), a blockbuster of 760 pages, is Pynchon's masterpiece to date. It is a hilariously wacky thriller whose inept detectives are scientists and psychologists trying to discover why a German V-2 rocket (gravity's rainbow) invariably strikes one of the many spots in London where the villainous American Air Force lieutenant, Tyrone Slothrop, has scored sexually: what is the connection between love and death?

Key 81   Alice Walker (1944–)

OVERVIEW   *Alice Walker is an African-American and a feminist. Her fiction draws upon the black experience in the American South and by creating strong women characters of near-heroic achievement, endows the African-American woman with a new identity, both distinct and admirable. In 1982 she won the American Book Award and the Pulitzer Prize for her novel* The Color Purple.

Themes: The strength, integrity, and wisdom of the black matriarch; the brutality and irresponsibility of the male within the underprivileged black family; white oppression and exploitation; the folk heritage of Southern blacks; issues of the womens' movement: sexism, rape, abortion, economic injustice.

Fictional method: Alice Walker writes in the tradition of realism modified by impressionism and muted symbolism. *The Color Purple* (1982) adopts the epistolary method of the earliest English novelists by telling its story partly through the letters of its heroine.

Meridian (1976): The story of a young black woman of the deep South, Meridian, whose choice of an independent life involves her in the civil rights movement of the '60s. In the urban North she rejects a part in the guerilla violence and comes home with the self-knowledge gained by her part in the struggle.

The Color Purple (1982): Celie suffers the poverty, racism, sexual abuse, and ignorance of a sharecropper family. Through strength of character she endures it all and rises in the end to a serene accommodation to her existence and restoration to those she loves.

"Everyday Use": This story evokes the strong matriarch in the subtitle, "for your grandmama." The visit of a superficially Africanized daughter to her mother and younger sister living in isolated rural poverty contrasts the attitudes of the sisters toward two heirloom quilts: African heritage as mere display vs. heritage for "everyday use."

Key 82   Theodore Roethke (1908–63)

OVERVIEW   *Roethke is a Modernist poet of the "second generation." His importance and the high quality of his poetry is suggested by Robert Lowell's poem "For Theodore Roethke," in which Lowell calls him, "The ocean's anchor, our high tide."*

Ideas: Roethke is in the direct line of American poetry that includes Emerson and Whitman. Like them, he is a transcendental poet who
- Sought God in nature.
- Believed feeling a more reliable source of truth than thought.
- Aimed at transcending the chaos of experience in a quest for oneness with the cosmos.

Poetic method: Roethke avoided talking about his subjects and instead presented in dramatic fashion the subject itself. The high seriousness of almost all his poems is frequently seasoned with wit and humor.
- Much of his most important poetry sets forth in often private imagery the origins of intense emotional anguish. His symbolism, generally drawn from nature, is complex. His poetry, as a consequence, is difficult.
- He wrote in a wide variety of forms, from compact stanzas through free verse to long-cadenced varieties of traditional structures.

Poems and themes:
- In "Cuttings (later)" the poet combines the theme of fertility in nature with the theme of physical and psychological regression: he *becomes* the cuttings struggling to put down roots and through pure empathy reexperiences his own birth and ("I quail") its psychological trauma.
- In a much more extended treatment of the theme of regression (found also in "Night Crow"), "Unfold! Unfold!" takes the poet back along the evolutionary process to his pre-human antecedents and forward from there through infancy and the psychological wounds of childhood to their tentative resolution in a series of proverb-like assertions.
- The themes of love and the joy of sex are set against the themes of aging and death in "I Knew a Woman," where Roethke's talent for combining humor and profundity shows the aging poet delightedly following the lead of the young woman who makes him feel both immortal and keenly aware of his own mortality.

Key 83   Elizabeth Bishop (1911–1979)

OVERVIEW   *Elizabeth Bishop began publishing poetry in 1946, at the end of the Modernist era. She writes within a narrow range, rarely treating love and death directly, and avoiding serious metaphysical speculation, politics, and social issues.*

Tone: Her poems are written with a dispassion toward life that finds her, in Whitman's phrase, "both in and out of the game."
- She is free of sentimentality and self-pity.
- Thus disburdened, she fills her poems with arresting descriptions of nature rich in color, astonishing the reader by revealing beauty habitually overlooked.
- She treats our lives with a detachment that is consistently ironical, cool, gently comical, iconoclastic, and smilingly deflating.

Poetic method: The forms of the poems the student encounters are about equally divided between free verse (always closely controlled) and rhymed verse that distances itself from traditional rhythms and orthodox rhyme schemes.
- The frequently anthologized villanelle "One Art" is an exception to the foregoing and to the characteristic dispassion and avoidance of self-pity.
- Almost all of the poems tell a story.

Themes:

- The intersection of nature with the things of mankind: "the fat brown bird / who sings above the broken gas pump," ("Questions of Travel"); our fire balloons that accidentally leave the burned armadillo "a weak mailed fist / clenched ignorant against the sky!" ("The Armadillo"); the fish "with...five big hooks / grown firmly in his mouth," ("The Fish").

- Beauty unexpected: "the pool of bilge / where oil had spread a rainbow" ("The Fish"); the herring scales that plaster a wheelbarrow "with creamy iridescent coats of mail, / with small iridescent flies crawling on them" ("At the Fishhouses"); and between the feet of the "Sandpiper," "millions of grains...black, white, tan, and gray, / mixed with quartz grains, rose and amethyst".

- Correspondences between the physical and the spiritual: the "Seascape" that assimilates herons to angels, mangrove roots to Gothic arches, bird-droppings on leaves to illuminated scripture, a jumping fish to a spray on a church tapestry, a "skeletal lighthouse" to a Calvinistic clergyman; the moose, looming "grand, otherworldly" in the road before the bus, that creates among the passengers a "sweet sensation of joy"; in "The Bight," the gas blue water vaporizes into marimba music, the dredge plays off-beat claves, stove-in skiffs become unanswered letters, allowing the poet to pun "The bight is littered with old correspondences."

Key 84   Robert Lowell (1917–1977)

OVERVIEW   *Lowell is foremost among those post World War II poets designated "confessional." Beginning his career in the 1940s under New Critical influence, he moved toward the confessional mode, which became dominant in* Life Studies *(1959) and continued to the end of his life. Rejecting his aristocratic New England family, he went to prison as a conscientious objector in World War II and joined the march on the Pentagon protesting the Vietnam War. His later poems draw on his family, treating their lives with realism, candor, and compassion. They "recover for poetry the territory it had surrendered to the novel."*

Method: Throughout his career Lowell used free verse and prose poetry together with a wide variety of stanzaic and rhymed forms—even sonnet sequences and couplets in iambic pentameter. Aiming to lay bare his heart, he chose the form best suited to his task.

Themes: Life itself—the casual, the random, the domestic, the ordinary; oedipal conflicts, marital conflicts, mental breakdowns; the Puritan heritage stained by greed, New England families ruined; Old Testament anger, Christianity's failures and potential for redeeming the world: revelation and apocalypse.

Poems: Two poems show Lowell fusing the personal and the public:
- "The Quaker Graveyard in Nantucket," an elegy for Lowell's war-drowned sailor cousin and a passionate denunciation in surreal imagery of war and man's fight with God, prophesying a distant peace when the world comes of its own will to "Calvary's Cross."
- "For the Union Dead": the Boston Aquarium is a memory of time past, now boarded up and empty of those symbols of eternal life, water and fish. Beside it, where corrupt politicians excavate for a civic garage, the adjacent Statehouse trembles for its lost virtue, and a monument to men dead in the cause of human brotherhood must be propped to survive "the garage's earthquake."
- "Epilogue": Offers Lowell's rationale for the realism and unflinching candor of the poems of self-revelation that comprise his work beginning with *Life Studies*. Its final lines: "We are poor passing facts, / warned by that to give / each figure in the photograph / his living name."

Key 85   Gwendolyn Brooks (1917–   )

OVERVIEW   *Drawing upon her experience in the black ghettoes of Chicago, Brooks published her first book of poems,* A Street in Bronzeville, *in 1945. Although they are rich in ethnic content, the poems were written on the principle that all human experience is essentially the same despite differences in the circumstances of life. They are shrewd, empathetic, concerned, often wryly humorous, realistic, reflecting a personal response to particular events. The concept of poetry governing* Bronzeville *was continued in* Annie Allen *(1949), the book which brought a Pulitzer Prize for the first time to a black writer. In the 1960s, however, Brooks became aware of the militancy of young black poets. Beginning with* In the Mecca *(1968) her poems became increasingly engaged with black social goals, including those of black feminists.*

Poems and themes:
- The gritty reality of black poverty that stifles dreams is the theme of "Kitchenette Building," but the light touch of humor with which it ends shows unembittered courage.
- The theme of black poverty recurs in "The Bean Eaters" and in "The Mother" with its burden of love for lives literally aborted.
- The theme, compassionately expressed, of the self-destructiveness of young blacks, appears in "A Song for the Front Yard," in "We Real Cool," and in "The Blackstone Rangers."
- Brooks does not often write satire, but in "Lovers of the Poor" she attacks with bitter irony the white "Ladies from the Ladies' Betterment League" for their unloving charity that cringes before the wretched realities of black tenement existence.
- Less angry satire is present in "The White Troops Had Their Orders But the Negroes Looked Like Men," and "The Chicago *Defender* Sends a Man to Little Rock."
- A new theme emerges in the late poem "To the Diaspora," where Brooks informs young blacks in America that they are indeed "Afrika...the Black continent," but optimistically declares that "some sun" of social ameliorization has touched them and beneath its light and warmth they have "...work to be done to be done to be done."

Key 86 Richard Wilbur (1921–   )

OVERVIEW   *Richard Wilbur is one of the "New Formalists," standing closer to the high Modernists who preceded him than to the poets of extreme self-revelation ("confessional poets") contemporary with him. Like Robert Frost, Wilbur finds that a poem creates a moment of order within the world's surrounding chaos. His poems are skillfully wrought, formal, lucid, witty, impersonal, and often charming. At their center there is usually a thought, familiar but delightfully arresting because freshly expressed.*

Poetic method: Wilbur's poems are cast in predetermined stanzaic forms, his lines in regular rhythms. Within his forms, he works with skill and elegance. His diction is likewise formal, sometimes intentionally old-fashioned. He has so far not been concerned with long poems or linked sequences of poems but rather has concentrated on the individual lyric.

Themes and poems:
- We are reminded in "The Death of a Toad" that nature and human artifice (the toad, the mower, and the mown lawn) are, alas, destructively linked. Another consequence of the profound difference between human kind and other nature is the theme of "Year's End"—the enduring beauty of death in nature can only be found in human death when it is transfigured by "the tapestries of afterthought," that is, by art.
- The relationship between art and nature is again treated in "Ceremony." There the lady, queenly, ceremonious, and artificial, painted in her tiger-striped blouse against foliage, evokes "most tigers in the wood" by demonstrating the power of art to declare our dominion over nature.
- The theme of humanly perceived correspondences between images in nature—meadow to lake, Queen Anne's Lace to water lilies— are "Beautiful Changes," but beauty itself changes its ambience by interaction with other beauty, and humankind can heighten beauty by introducing an ethical element: "Your hands hold roses always in a way that says / They are not only yours."

Key 87   James Dickey (1923–   )

OVERVIEW   *Dickey belongs to the Romantic tradition that discovers in nature clues to the ultimate realities of the human existence. Some of his best poems arise out of mystical experiences that unite his consciousness with river, marsh, trees, animals, and stars, in ways that assure him of resurrection and immortality through art.*

Poetic method: In his first phase, Dickey wrote mainly in short unrhymed lines, markedly rhythmic, with dactyls predominating. In the mid-1960s he began more and more to extend his line and diminish the distinctness of its rhythm.
- Thereafter, space between phrases and lines, supplanted much punctuation.
- Throughout, he has written narrative poetry in the broadest sense, reminding us that he is the author of two successful novels, *Deliverance* (1970), and *Alnilam* (1987).

Themes and poems: Mankind is not distinct from the rest of nature but can become one with it and through this merging have intimations of immortality. *Examples:* "Inside the River," where the poet is tempted to "Enter the sea like a winding wind"; "In the Mountain Tent," which ends with the assertion, "I shall rise from the dead"; and "The Salt Marsh," where he says of the swaying grasses, "nothing prevents your bending / With them... / In their marvelous spiritual walking / Everywhere, anywhere."
- A variant on this theme appears in "The Lifeguard," where the lifeguard-poet resurrects the drowned child by the power of the imagination and immortalizes him in art.
- He celebrates erotic love, exuberantly in "Cherrylog Road," with tender irony in "Adultery," terrifyingly in "Falling."
- His experience as a World War II night-fighter pilot is reflected with compassion in *Helmets* (1964) and elsewhere.

Key 88   The "Beat" Poets:

Alan Ginsberg and Gary Snyder

OVERVIEW   *Within the "beat" counterculture, the poet is a central figure, a guru of sorts, whose style of living, as much as his poetry, challenges social values and offers moral and spiritual instruction. "Beat" suggests beat down and/or beatific.*

Themes: Freedom, the rejection of middle-class life (often by "dropping out"), the ideal of a classless world, uninhibited sex, ecological preservation, the wisdom of beliefs outside mainline Western religions (especially Zen Buddhism), drugs and the overthrow of rational values, transcendence and ecstasy, communalism, primitivism, and a return to nature.

Poetic methods: Ginsberg writes in free verse with the diction and breath-patterns of ordinary speech.
- Startling adjective-noun pairings frequently seize the reader's attention, however, and the breath patterns can extend a single sentence of long lines in parallel structure for pages.
- The often oracular manner is checked by irony and self-deprecation, the seriousness tempered by humor.
- Like Ginsberg, Snyder writes a free verse shaped by the demands of the poem itself, allowing it to grow as an organism according to its nature. His manner, however, is quiet with the matter-of-factness of actual experience directly transcribed.

Representative poems:
- Ginsberg's best poem is the influential "Howl." It denounces in more than 100 long lines of angry hyperbole the life-blighting effects of American civilization on the minds and spirits of the young. The poet surrealistically describes the frantic attempt of "the best minds" of his generation to find in restless movement, in drugs, alcohol, and orgiastic sex, alleviation from the pain inflicted by American militarism, industrial impersonality, urban squalor, economic greed, and so on.
- Gary Snyder's "Riprap" by contrast finds its imagery in nature and is wholly metaphoric: the poem is the title poem of a volume of Snyder's verse whose individual poems "like rocks / placed solid" might provide riprap for our lives as we struggle for footing in the slippery places of our existence.

Key 89   John Ashbery (1927–   )

OVERVIEW   *Ashbery is perhaps the most important American poet of the present day. His meditative poems ask the reader to struggle to find their "meaning," but there are rewards all along the way in brilliant imagery, active language, and even ideas. Unfortunately there is as yet no substantial criticism to help the reader.*

Themes: Time; the nature of reality; the elusiveness of experience; the terror inherent in our awareness of transition, change, loss.

Method: Departing from a concrete fact or event, the poems move forward by evoking a succession of associated images and ideas. A wide variety of forms are employed, from the traditional through open forms to the prose poem.

Poems:
- "Instruction Manual": the poet's mind wanders from the task of writing an instruction manual to take a colorful excursion through Guadalajara, a city he has never visited, but vividly imagined, returning at the end to the task.
- "The Desperado" declares Ashbery's preoccupation with the dissipation of experience, the kaleidoscopic replacement of event by event. "Now all will be gone," he laments, and instead of cultivating young thoughts, he braces himself against the imagined gray future.
- "The Lonedale Operator" is a prose poem whose events raise unanswered questions about Time and Reality. Together the events and questions create uneasy emotional states.

Key 90   Anne Sexton (1928–1975)

OVERVIEW   *Like her contemporaries Sylvia Plath and Adrienne Rich, Anne Sexton made her poems out of the literal anguish of her life. The madness that overtook her from time to time seems to have been a refuge from the forces that made her life intolerable. Her ultimate refuge was suicide. Her poems gained a large audience among the many women who found in her verse an expression of their own perplexities.*

Themes: Familial relationships—parents and children, wives and husbands; sex, infidelity, madness, guilt, suicide, and death.

Poems:
- "Her Kind" casts the poet as a witch, presenting her in three aspects: first, the night rider, abnormal, alienated, mad, dreaming evil for the community, touchingly aware that consequently she "is not a woman, quite"; second, a power humanizing rude nature and with eccentric insistence making the odd all even, her intentions misunderstood and probably feared; third, a witch convicted by the community carried to torture and the stake, still defiant and morally unvanquished.
- "The Truth the Dead Know" is the truth that death is forever, that they lie buried beyond our blessing. Although the sea swings in on our seaside escape, like the iron gate of a cemetery and the wind off the waves "falls in like stones" from a graveyard, "when we touch, we enter touch entirely" and know that in sexual love we inhabit a country at the greatest distance possible from the dead.

Key 91 Adrienne Rich (1929–   )

OVERVIEW *Adrienne Rich in her poems candidly explores her emotional life, but less sensationally than other so-called "confessional" poets. In the mid-1970s she turned her attention more toward the experiences of other women and wrote to raise their consciousness on feminist issues. Today she is foremost among the radical feminist poets of America.*

Themes: The quest for self-knowledge, dissatisfaction with a woman's traditional roles, fear of being false to one's authentic self, the painful struggle to resist yielding to the expectations of others, the joy of finding lost mother-love, love of self, and love of another like oneself in homosexual union.

Poetic method: Beginning her career in 1951 under the influence of the New Formalists, by the 1960s she had abandoned their meter and stanza for verse that found its effects in extended metaphor, the juxtaposition of sounds, and the rhythmic manipulation of the line.

"Aunt Jennifer's Tigers": An early poem in Neo-Formalist style that sees dead Aunt Jennifer as an artist-figure whose marriage was a frightening ordeal "she was mastered by." The tigers she embroidered, however, "Will go on prancing, proud and unafraid."

"Upper Broadway": Uses the metaphor of a leafbud in an airshaft reaching for end—of—winter's light to express the poet's striving toward change and growth. The poet sees herself as a "slippered crone inching on icy streets / reaching into wire trashbaskets pulling out / what was thrown away and infinitely precious" to suggest the creative process.

"Diving into the Wreck": Uses the metaphor of scuba diving to explore the submerged self and with the "merman in his body armor" investigate the wreck of their lives "the damage that was done / and the treasures that prevail," themselves "the half-destroyed instruments / that once held to a course / the water-eaten log / the fouled compass," of a marriage that lost its way.

Key 92   Sylvia Plath (1932–63)

OVERVIEW   *Sylvia Plath is a post-Modernist whose most important poems, though often blunt and brutal, meet the requirement of the New Critics for complex emotions expressed with ambiguity and ambivalence. Their range of reference is confined to the poet's own feelings, which, though intense and even excessive, are always held under artistic control. Ariel (1965) is her most important volume of verse. The anguish there confessed would seem to account for the poet's suicide at the age of 31.*

Themes: The poems express frustration at the difficulty of self-fulfillment, the choking restrictions of domestic life, hatred of men, the father, and the husband, murderous rage, the death wish, horror at the memory of the Nazi holocaust and at the prospect of nuclear war, disgust, sickness, and torment.

Poems:
- "Lady Lazarus" is a sardonic statement of the poet's intention to attempt by incineration suicide for the third time, treating the matter as a performance where the vulgar crowd will applaud her as she rises from the ashes "with my red hair / And…eat men like air."
- In "Ariel" she recounts a ride into the dawn, the rider becoming one with the horse, sweeping through briars that tear away old restrictions, old traditions, becoming naked as Godiva of "feudal" limitations, merging with the dew-laden wind, the horse now pure spirit, "suicidal" into the flaming sun.
- "Daddy" is a frantic, hysterical denunciation of a father who is given as a jack-booted brute, a Nazi torturer, a devil. Desperate love is beneath the shrieking, spitting hatred, her attempted suicide at 10 and again at 20 expressing her heartbreak at being rejected. An imagined stake through the heart of this vampire kills with one gesture both him and his surrogate, the poet's husband. The poem avoids self-pitying sentimentality by the fury of its utterance.

GLOSSARY

allegory A narrative in which different elements have one or more symbolic meanings in addition to their literal significance.

allusion A passing reference, often to a literary work.

archetype A model or supreme example.

autobiography An account of a person's life written by that person.

beats, beat generation A group flourishing in the 1950s that emphasized mysticism and rejection of social taboos.

blank verse Verse written in unrhymed five-stress lines.

Calvinism A doctrine emphasizing predestination and strict discipline.

chronicle A historical record presented in chronological order.

colloquial Having to do with ordinary, informal speech.

convention A traditional or accepted way of doing or expressing something.

counterculture Opposition to the prevailing culture of the time, specifically referring to the rebellious youth of the 1960s and 1970s.

dialect The speech of a particular region or class.

diction The choice of words.

dramatic monologue A poem in the form of a speech by a specific character.

ellipsis An omission, generally of some word or words.

epistolary novel A novel written in the form of letters between the characters, popular in the 18th century.

essay A short prose composition, generally on a single topic.

feminism Attention to topics and themes of particular concern to women, frequently emphasizing injustices.

free verse Verse written without strict meter or rhyme.

genteel Overly polite and seeking to avoid any possibly offensive language or topics.

grotesque Bizarrely fantastic.

hyperbole Overstatement for dramatic or comic effect.

imagery Representation of things or creatures, often for emotional or symbolic effect.

imagism A twentieth-century school of poets who believed that the impact of a poem should be conveyed through images.

impressionism The theory that natural objects should be described as they immediately strike the observer without conscious or deliberate selection or elaboration.

irony Something that conveys a contradictory meaning in addition to the literal meaning.

juxtapose To place words or images close to one another, frequently for ironic purposes.

Latinate Derived from Latin, frequently referring to words that are elaborate and unusual.

local color Picturesque and idiosyncratic detail about a particular region or location.

Lost Generation The self-consciously disillusioned generation that came of age after World War I, in the 1920s.

lyric A short, song-like poem expressing the poet's own thoughts and feelings.

metaphor A figure of speech comparing one object to another.

meter The regular rhythm of a line of poetry.

Modernism An international movement, dominating the first half of the twentieth century, that rejected tradition, valued experimentation, and emphasized myth and the unconscious mind.

narrative A story, either fictional or true.

Naturalism A literary movement that shares with Realism its attention to the speech and behavior of the present, but that considers people's behavior to be determined by social and economic forces beyond human control.

neoclassicism Literary movement, particularly important in the eighteenth century, that tried to emulate the standards of classical Greece and Rome, emphasizing reason and decorum.

objectivity The effort on the part of the author to maintain a neutral attitude toward the characters and events portrayed.

oral tradition Unwritten lore learned by memory and passed down through generations.

orthodox Generally approved or accepted.

parable A story told to illustrate a moral point.

persona The character or personality adopted by the author in narrating a work.

propaganda A work whose primary purpose is to put forth a specific point of view.

pun A play on words that sound alike or nearly alike but have different meanings.

Puritanism A religious movement of the sixteenth and seventeenth centuries that sought to "purify" the Church of England. The term is frequently used to refer to a strictly, even rigidly moral attitude.

Realism Characteristic of the second half of the nineteenth century, literary Realism seeks to record accurately the speech and behavior of ordinary people and to depict life honestly, without recourse to melodrama or improbable events.

regionalist An author whose writings are closely tied to a particular section of the country.

rhetoric The use of language to influence people emotionally. Frequently, the use of overblown language.

rhyme The repetition of the final sounds of words, either at the ends of lines of poetry or within a line (internal rhyme).

romance A story with heroic, exotic elements.

Romanticism A literary school emphasizing imagination and emotion.

satire A literary work making fun of the follies of humanity or society.

sentimentality A superficial appeal to emotion.

sermon A discourse intended to give spiritual or religious instruction.

slave narrative A type of narrative popular in the nineteenth century, recounting both the horrors of slavery and the opportunities that come with escape and freedom.

supernaturalism Belief in divine or other non-natural influence on human affairs.

syllogism A strictly constructed logical argument.

symbol An image that represents or stands for something in addition to its literal meaning.

syntax The grammatical structure of sentences and phrases.

tall tale A story filled with exaggerated incidents, generally comic.

theocracy A system of government in which the religious leaders are also the political leaders.

transcendentalism The belief that the visible world, imaginatively and intuitively perceived, provides hints of the invisible, eternal world.

typography The way a poem is set up and printed on a page.

verse Poetry, especially when in regular metrical form, as opposed to prose.

versification Putting into metrical form.

vignette A brief illustrative story.

INDEX